THE
CRUCIFIED
NATION

To Jeremy, Melanie and Julia
My grandchildren

THE
CRUCIFIED
NATION

A Motif in
Modern
Nationalism

ALAN DAVIES

sussex
ACADEMIC
PRESS

BRIGHTON • *PORTLAND*

2 4 6 8 10 9 7 5 3 1

First published in 2008 by
SUSSEX ACADEMIC PRESS
PO Box 139
Eastbourne BN24 9BP

and in the United States of America by
SUSSEX ACADEMIC PRESS
920 NE 58th Ave   Suite 300
Portland, Oregon 97213-3786

British Library Cataloguing in Publication Data
A CIP catalogue record for this book is available from the British Library.

Library of Congress Cataloging-in-Publication Data
Davies, Alan.
 The crucified nation : a motif in modern nationalism / Alan
  Davies.
  p. cm.
  Includes bibliographical references and index.
  ISBN 978-1-84519-273-0 (hb : alk. paper)
 1. Nationalism—Cross-cultural studies. 2. Nationalism—
Religious aspects—Christianity. I. Title.

 JC311.D345 2008
 320.54—dc22

                                                   2007047674

Typeset and designed by SAP, Brighton & Eastbourne.
Printed by TJ International, Padstow, Cornwall.
This book is printed on acid-free paper.

Contents

Preface and Acknowledgments

The title of this study was suggested by a chance comment made by a colleague several years ago in the Senior Common Room at Victoria College in the University of Toronto. An expert in eastern European history, he alluded to Polish nationalism, about which I then knew nothing, and the old belief in Poland as the Christ-nation or the Christ of the nations. The remark intrigued me, for I have long been interested in the subject of nationalism and as a student of religion I have long been aware of its religious dimensions. Moreover, the spectacle of an innocent and virtuous nation under assault by less innocent and less virtuous powers was very much in the news at the time of my common room conversation. A chain of reflection started in my mind, and this book is the result. It was not easy to write since the scope of my project forced me into areas in which I am far from competent and such ventures are always hazardous. For one thing, I do not know a single word of Polish, Gaelic or Arabic, a serious handicap in the scholarly study of Polish, Irish and Palestinian nationalism, although also an advantage since the less one knows about a subject the easier it is to write about it. Providentially, I was able to cover my deficiencies by enlisting the services of those better informed, although I cannot foist the responsibility for errors and misjudgments on others; they are my responsibility alone. Much poetry has been cited, since poets are often the most eloquent voices of nationalist sentiment; however, novelists, dramatists, historians, philosophers and preachers have also contributed their literary wares. If I have simplified too much and condensed too much material, ignoring nuances as well as significant details, I can only offer my apologies, but a full account of five nationalisms in five countries was not my intent and lies beyond my powers in any case. Instead, I have settled for a series of relatively brief depictions, two of which (the chapters on France and Germany) owe part of their provenance to one of my earlier ventures in the history of ideas.[1] Some of the same *dramatis personae* reappear with a few embellishments.

Like all such comparative studies, my survey is selective and necessarily unfinished. Other countries doubtless fit into the same broad pattern as Poland, France, Germany, Ireland and Palestine. I have chosen Poland because of the centrality of the crucified nation motif in Polish nationalism, France and Germany because of the signal importance of these nations in European and world history, Ireland because of my own Irish descent (my maternal grandfather came from Cavan), and Palestine because of its haunting presence in the fiery furnace of the contemporary Middle East. Moreover, as I take pains to point out, certain common roots connect Polish, French, German, Irish and Palestinian nationalism. Some other nationalisms and incipient nationalisms of a similar nature are mentioned in my concluding chapter. If these preliminary comments suffice as a foreword, any further apologia can be postponed for the moment. The text, I believe, explains itself.

It only remains to acknowledge my debts. To Tamara Trojanowska, Eric Jennings, Martin Rumscheidt, David Wilson, Jay Macpherson, Solomon Nigosian and James Reilly, who have read and criticized separate chapters, and to William Callahan and my old friend Terence Anderson who have read and criticized the entire manuscript, I am deeply grateful. All have allowed me to infringe on their time, and I cannot find adequate words to express my thanks. I am also grateful to Sussex Academic Press for being interested in my ideas and for making their publication possible.

The author and publisher gratefully acknowledge the following for permission to reproduce copyright material: Salma K. Jayyusi (editor), 'Abd al-Rahim Mahmud, "Call of the Motherland"; Mu'in Bsisu, "The Vinegar Cup"; Hanan Mikha'il Ashrawi, "Metamorphosis", in *Anthology of Modern Palestinian Literature*, Columbia University Press, 1992. Salma K. Jayyusi (editor), 'Abd al-Rahim Mahmud, "The Aqsa Mosque", in *Trends and Movements in Modern Arabic Poetry*, Volume I, Brill, NV, 1977. The publishers apologize for any errors or omissions in the above list and would be grateful to be notified of any corrections that should be incorporated in the next edition or reprint of this book.

ALAN DAVIES
Victoria College, Toronto

Note

1 Alan Davies, *Infected Christianity: A Study of Modern Racism*, Montreal & Kingston: McGill-Queen's University Press, 1988.

THE
CRUCIFIED
NATION

A Motif in
Modern
Nationalism

Introduction

On September 11, 2001, the unthinkable happened. That impregnable bastion, the United States of America, suffered an attack on its own soil at the hands of hidden forces, traumatizing a nation used to thinking of itself as a beacon of light and liberty, a model of virtue and innocence in a world of vice and guilt. It was not difficult, in light of this conviction, to interpret the destruction of the World Trade Center in New York in cosmic terms. Surely the assault was motivated by a hatred of American freedom on the part of those who detest freedom and therefore detest its greatest earthly manifestation. One could step further and speak of the 'Passion of America,' as a Canadian commentator has noted,[1] for biblical language and biblical metaphors come readily in a society largely formed by Protestant and puritan ideals. In this context, of course, the term 'passion' refers to the fateful final days of Jesus in Jerusalem as they are recounted in the gospels and recited during Holy Week when Christians trace the footsteps of their messiah from his entry into the city to his arrest, trial and subsequent crucifixion.[2] It is therefore an emotionally charged word, replete with lofty spiritual claims and consonant with the sense of special status (election) and messianic mission invoked by every American president, usually at his inauguration. However, the American national myth with its core belief in manifest destiny has never been based on feelings of national immolation: the proverbial 'nation on the cross.' Dark obsessions with collective victimization – the graphic suffering servant of Deutero-Isaiah who is led like a lamb to the slaughter★ – are not characteristic of American nationalism which, like British nationalism, generally prefers to sound a note of self-confidence and impending triumph as the elect nation proceeds on its civilizing mission hand in hand with God.[3] Until September 11, 2001, no Americans or non-Americans would likely have described the United States as a crucified nation. Not even December 7, 1941 (Pearl Harbor), President Franklin Delano

★ Isaiah 52:13–53:12.

1

Roosevelt's notorious 'day of infamy,' seems to have inspired such a designation.

Are things different now? Has the soul of the American republic changed? I beg the question, but an affirmative answer is not inconceivable. If a foreign dimension, one of suffering messianism, has truly insinuated itself into the national psyche as the result of the assault by al-Qaida on the "last best hope of earth" (Abraham Lincoln), something new has certainly transpired. The Passion of America then joins the Passion of Poland, the Passion of France, the Passion of Germany, the Passion of Ireland, the Passion of Palestine and the other national passions in the roster of crucified nations – crucified in their own eyes and sometimes in the eyes of others – that crowd the annals of modern history. As I shall argue, these passion narratives are not only vainglorious in their moral and spiritual claims but actually demonic and dangerous in the blindness and one-sidedness they usually nourish, even if they serve to rally oppressed peoples during their tribulations. They represent a Christian or quasi-Christian variation on the biblical or quasi-biblical theme of the chosen nation that, in one form or another, appears in virtually every expression of political nationalism in the modern world, including countries with other religious traditions. This is a book about nationalism, but not in a conceptual or analytical sense; many better known works by more famous authorities exist to trace its history and explore its roots. In particular, I bow the knee before Sir Isaiah Berlin, Elie Kedourie, Hans Kohn, Ernest Gellner, Benedict Anderson, Eric Hobsbawm, Louis L. Snyder and a score of others. Their influence is omnipresent in my study, especially that of Berlin, Kedourie and Kohn.

My personal views on the subject emerge as the chapters unfold. I accept the notion, expounded by most of the above, that nationalism, the cult or ideology of the nation, is distinct (although not completely distinct) from patriotism, a more simple and rudimentary emotion. Nationalism, like its cousin racism, is the creature of modernity and the offspring of the evolving and increasingly secular mind of the West. As Benedict Anderson has famously suggested, it is a work of the imagination, meaning that nations in the final analysis are really fictions invented by fertile and frequently poetic brains.[4] It is not the nation that produces nationalism but rather nationalism that posits the nation. Had the nationalist sentiment never arisen, nations themselves would never have arisen in their contemporary sense as distinctive and *sui generis* communities, a fact easily and conveniently forgotten. Nationalism, however, which was spawned by intellectuals, gathered up and drew together all the emerging forces of the dawning modern age in search of new modes of being, especially the struggle for political freedom and human self-realization.[5] Part of this search involved the quest for proper modes of distinguishing the peoples of the earth from each other, giving birth not only to the modern nation but also to the modern nation-state and thus to all of the troubles that arise when nations and states do not perfectly coincide. A product of European and Western civilization, nationalism has now spread to all corners of the world: the Middle East, Asia, Africa and even the islands of the seven seas. Few places are left – perhaps the small isolated Himalayan kingdom of Bhutan is one example – that remain unaffected by its revolutionary dynamism.

The word nationalism or *nationalisme* is a modern coinage. According to one (French) source, it was first employed by Augustin Barruel, an exiled French priest in flight from the Reign of Terror in Paris in his uncomplimentary *Mémoires* (1798) regarding the Jacobins and their radical transformation of the social and political order.[6] If so it entered the lexicon at the close of the eighteenth century. New words are tokens of new feelings and new concepts and, once established, are not easily displaced, although they are subject to amendment in the course of time. Nationalism has acquired a series of meanings including political sovereignty, territorial rights, language, culture, religion, ethnicity and even race. In one form or another all of these elements can be found in every nationalist movement, although not always in equal measure. All are present in the five nationalisms that constitute our study, and all are mentioned; however, because of the Christ-nation motif so fervently promoted by certain Polish, French, German, Irish and Palestinian nationalists, it is the religious component that commands the most attention in the pages that follow. This is a book about religion as well as about nationalism; in fact, it is a book about Christianity, although in an indirect fashion. The image of the crucified nation, of course, has a Christian derivation, which poses a special problem for Christians because of the manner in which the churches have so often implicated themselves in nationalist and ultra-nationalist politics. However, the notion of nationhood itself as defined by nationalist ideologues – Emmanuel Joseph Sieyès is a good example[7] – also assumes a sacred character in its spiritual pretensions and the devotion it commands, no matter how secular its political and constitutional fabric. As we shall see, the French Republic is a particularly potent case.

These themes will re-emerge in the concluding chapter, and I will reserve my critical judgments until that point Today, in the often violent clash of nations, religions and cultures, when too many too readily, as Michael Ignatieff has written,[8] champion holy wars and exalt old martyrdoms that license every conceivable crime in the name of "nation, people, rights and freedom," the need for serious self-criticism is more than evident. My book, I trust, will be read as an exercise in Christian self-criticism as well as a general moral tract for the times. Even in Canada, the country where I live, a country where nationalism is more regional than 'national,' a country that values compromise above most other political virtues, a country that prides itself on its reasonableness and seldom indulges in public displays of patriotic excess, the crucifixion motif has demonstrated its appeal. In her book *Mother of Heroes, Mothers of Martyrs* Suzanne Evans alludes to a now mostly forgotten 32-inch high bronze statue cast in 1918 entitled "Canada's Golgotha" depicting the alleged literal crucifixion of a Canadian soldier by German soldiers during the Second Battle of Ypres (1915).[9] The crucified Canadian, nailed to a barn door, is shown enduring the jeers of his Hunnish crucifiers. Whether the crucifixion was factual or fictional – atrocities do occur in war but most probably it was fictional – has never been determined despite several investigations. Whether true or false, however, it seems to have served the propagandistic ends for which it was designed. Such was the super-patriotic mood of the epoch and, while moods can and do change, it is always possible for them to change back as well. Moreover, no nation is immune to the lure of self-glorification, and certainly no nationalism.

Yet nationalism is not a constant; it can vary in intensity, waxing and waning in tandem with historical circumstance and other factors in the course of time. Monolithic impressions are misleading and it would be a mistake to conclude that men such as Adam Mickiewicz or Victor Hugo or Patrick Pearse spoke for all or even most of their compatriots and fellow-nationals, or that the zealous German pastors of the Great War spoke for all Germans. Not only are many citizens of any nation not nationalists, but nationalists also are not all cut from the same cloth. At the same time, some lessons can be learned by tracing certain resemblances. What follows is the delineation of a single motif in five modern nationalisms: a common thread that runs through the intricate fabric of one of the most powerful ideologies of the contemporary world. As far as I know, no one else has probed the nationalist mind by pursuing the Christ-metaphor as far as I have attempted in the following pages. Whether or not I have managed to cast any light on its inner workings is for the reader to decide.

Notes

1 Rick Salutin, "The Passion of Christ and George Bush's America," *The Globe and Mail* (Toronto), February 27, 2004.
2 Mark 11–15 is the oldest extant account.
3 An exception to this statement is the special phenomenon of Black American nationalism.
4 Benedict Anderson, *Imagined Communities: Reflections on the Origin and Spread of Nationalism*, 1983.
5 See the splendid essay by John Hutchinson & Anthony D. Smith in their edited work *Nationalism*, Oxford: Oxford University Press, 1994, pp. 3–13.
6 Cf. Gregory Jusdanis, *The Necessary Nation*, Princeton: Princeton University Press, 2001, p. 18, fn. 1.
7 Emmanuel Joseph Sieyès, *Qu'est ce-que le Tiers État?*, 1789. See also Heinrich Schneider, "Patriotism and Nationalism," *Religion and Nationalism*, John Coleman and Miklós Tomka (editors), London: SCM Press, 1995, p. 38.
8 Michael Ignatieff, *Blood and Belonging: Journeys into the New Nationalism,* Harmondsworth: Viking Penguin, 1993, p. 39. Ignatieff is currently the deputy leader of the Liberal Party of Canada.
9 Suzanne Evans, *Mother of Heroes, Mothers of Martyrs: World War I and the Politics of Grief*, Montreal & Kingston: McGill–Queen's University Press, 2007, pp. 52, 54–56. The sculptor was Francis Derwent Wood.

I

The Crucified Nation
POLAND

The image of the crucified nation was conceived by and large during the high noon of European romanticism and popularized by the patriotic Polish poet Adam Mickiewicz (1798–1855). Remembered for his dashing career and assorted masterpieces, including the epic poem *Pan Tadeusz*, regarded by some literary historians as the finest jewel in Polish literature, Mickiewicz devoted a famous political tract *The Books of the Polish Nation and of the Polish Pilgrimage*★ to the cause of Polish freedom. It contains the following fable:

> . . . in idolatrous Europe there rose three rulers [i.e., Frederick the Great of Prussia, Catherine the Great of Russia, Maria Theresa of Austria] . . . But the Polish Nation alone did not bow down . . . And finally Poland said: 'Whosoever will come to me shall be free and equal, for I am FREEDOM' . . . the Kings when they heard of this were terrified in their hearts, and said . . . 'Come, let us slay this nation' . . . And they martyred the Polish Nation, and laid in its grave, and the kings cried out 'We have slain and buried Freedom' . . . the Polish Nation did not die . . . on the third day . . . the Nation shall rise, and free all the peoples of Europe from slavery.[1]

The poet's allusion is to the dismemberment of the once proud and independent Republic or Commonwealth of Poland † in three successive partitions from 1772 to 1795 by the three great powers of central and eastern Europe, Prussia, Austria and Russia. In their decision to devour

---

★ Ksiegi narodu polskiego i pielgrzymstwa polskiego.

† Although Poland had kings, it was called a republic or commonwealth (*Rzezpospolita*), since its kings were elected after the end of the Jagiellon dynasty in 1572.

their neighbour, the adjacent rulers only acted as arrogant leaders usually act when they possess the means to aggrandize themselves and when historical circumstances provide the opportunity. The past is full of examples, and so is the present. However, Poland was an unusual victim in certain respects. Because of its semi-democratic nature – democratic in the sense that its institutions were radical in comparison with most other European states – the Polish commonwealth had never been regarded with much favour by the presiding autocrats of the continent. When constitutional reforms of too liberal a nature for the latter to stomach were introduced in Warsaw in 1791, the fate of the Polish kingdom-republic was effectively sealed. Fearful of new political experiments, the absolute monarchs of the day took steps to prevent the banners of even a tepid liberalism from arising within their own borders in imitation of the Poles. *Realpolitik* prevailed and Polish independence was extinguished, but the clock of historical time could not be turned back as far as the forces of reaction desired.

The late eighteenth century was a time of bold new ideas, an age when unprecedented passions were stirring, many of them generated by the French Revolution of 1789. One was the idea of the nation (from the Latin *natio*), not, to be sure, an invention of the modern world but its special brainchild nonetheless. Although the word itself extends back to antiquity, its contemporary meaning was forged both by the Age of Reason and the subsequent romantic protest against rationalism. These twin intellectual currents brought the national idea to the forefront of European thought, thereby changing its character. Questions of national and cultural distinctiveness became a popular obsession in contemporary letters, of which David Hume's well-known essay "Of National Characters" is a good example. Nationalism, the cult or ideology of the nation, was born. From henceforth, declared one of its French progenitors, all citizens must be "melted into the national mass."[2]

According to one theory, this seismic shift was a result of the general fragmentation of time-honoured patterns of thought in the twilight of the Middle Ages.[3] As the European mind grew more secular, certain group ideas, including those of race and class, more or less submerged in earlier periods, rose to the surface and gained an autonomy that hitherto they had never possessed. The concept of nationhood was a case in point, a concept symbolized by new national (as opposed to dynastic) flags, new national anthems and various other tokens of collective identity. To those not trapped in feudalism, it was clear that the world was changing. Almost from the first hour of its political demise in 1795, the Polish national idea started to acquire a deeper and more potent significance: "Poland is not yet lost!" cried angry and rebellious Poles in a military marching song of the day that later became the Polish national anthem.[4] The seeds of resistance were sown early, and it was not long before they bore fruit. Because of their *avant-garde* civic traditions – the "democracy of the gentry" or "noble democracy"[5] – the Polish loyalists not only managed to survive the loss of their state but also to nourish and deepen their attachment to their national identity. The cost, however, was steep. Their ignominious fate and feelings of "bitter alienation" forced the Poles, more than most peoples, to live in a world of dreams and myths, nursing and cultivating an "imaginary mythologized history."[6] If nationalism is defined as homage to a nation rather than a king or feudal lord, Polish nationalism is as old if not older than French and German nationalism, despite the influence of both French and German intellectual forces on Polish thought.[7] In the case of Poland, however, the national idea was diminished by the fact that only the landed upper classes were defined as Polish, an oligarchic social order inherited from the old commonwealth. The lower classes, including the vast peasant population, were not so regarded, a state of affairs that crippled the glorious cause of national emancipation.

Adam Mickiewicz, the poet-apostle of Polish nationalism, was born after the final immolation of his country, but this inconvenient fact merely inflamed his *amor patriae*, his love of a Poland that he had never known since it had literally vanished from the map of Europe. Patriotic hopes were stirred briefly in his youth by Napoleon's military victories over Austria and Prussia, when, as a sop to Polish aspirations, a relatively small French-sponsored Duchy of Warsaw was established with Russian consent in 1807. Despite its French flavour and some favourable concessions, the new mini-state was too insignificant to please its Polish citizens. The French emperor's days were numbered, however, and, after his second abdication in 1815, the Duchy of Warsaw was replaced by a new semi-autonomous Kingdom of Poland established by the Congress of Vienna (hence known as the 'Congress Kingdom'). Although located in the heart of the former commonwealth, the Congress Kingdom was a truncated domain and its king, in any case, was the Russian tsar. Both Alexander I and his successor Nicholas I paid insufficient heed to the rights and interests of their Polish subjects, especially Tsar Nicholas Alexander had more liberal reflexes. Their far from benign neglect led to a serious insurrection in Warsaw in 1830, a fateful and tumultuous year in European history. The November Uprising, which succeeded in dislodging the tsar from his Polish throne, failed nonetheless to re-establish Polish independence. After exciting a fresh outburst of nationalist fury, it was suppressed during the following year, and, as a punishment, the Polish constitution was suspended and the rebellious Poles were crushed under the Russian heel. A remorseless process of Russification began.

This unfortunate turn of events produced the Great Emigration, a mass flight of Polish refugees, including much of the intelligentsia (a word that the exiled Poles themselves may actually have coined), to the major cities of western Europe. It also produced a new flowering of Polish literature and Polish philosophy, much of which was written in exile. Mickiewicz himself was not part of the Great Emigration, having departed from his fatherland well before the uprising. As a university student in Vilna (Wilno), the young poet had embroiled himself in radical politics as a member of a subversive secret society, leading to a term in a Russian prison and, on release, five years of restriction from foreign travel. When finally allowed to leave Russia in 1829, his fortunes led him to Italy and Germany (Dresden), where he joined other Polish émigrés, only to move later to Paris, by this time (1832) the nerve centre of Polish national life and the home of some five thousand exiled Poles.[8] There the Polish Lord Byron, his head awash with romantic ideas, dreamt of his nation's liberation. There he composed the prose work cited above, with its messianic interpretation of Polish destiny and its even more daring designation of Poland as the Christ of the nations. This deeply emotional comparison between the crucified messiah and the crucified nation was immortalized also in his poetry:

> I see my nation bound, all Europe drags him on
>   And mocks at him:
> 'To the judgment hall!' - The multitude leads in the
>   guiltless man.
> Mouths, without hearts or hands, are judges here,
> And all shout, 'Gaul! – Let Gaul be judge!'
> Gaul found no fault in him – and washed his hands;
> And yet the kings shout, 'Judge him! Punish him!
> His blood shall be on us and on our children;
> Crucify Mary's son and loose Barabbas!
> He scorneth Caesar's crown: crucify him,
> Or we will say, thou art not Caesar's friend.'
> And Gaul delivered him unto the people -
> They led him forth – and then this innocent head
> Grew bloodstained from the mocking crown of thorns;
> They raised him up in sight of all the world -
> The people thronged to see – and Gaul cried out,

'Behold the free and independent nation!'

I see the cross. – O Lord, how long, how long
Must he still bear it? Lord, be merciful!
Strengthen thy servant lest he fall and die!
The cross has arms that shadow all of Europe,
Made of three withered peoples, like dead trees.
Now is my nation on the martyr's throne.
He speaks and says, 'I thirst,' and Rakus gives him
To drink of vinegar, and Borus, gall,
While Mother Freedom stands below and weeps.
And now a soldier hired in Muscovy
Comes forward with his pike and pierces him,
And from my guiltless nation blood has gushed . . .

O my beloved! He droops his dying head
And now in a loud voice he calls, 'My God,
My God, and why hast thou forsaken me'
                    And he is dead.[9]

These lines from *Dziady* or *Forefathers' Eve*, Part III, a poem that has been compared to Dante's *Divine Comedy*,[10] were written in Dresden in 1832 in a fit of "frenzied inspiration" following some kind of personal and mystical vision.[11] They should be read as an extended metaphor, a figurative personification of the Polish tragedy in religious or crypto-religious terms. In this passion drama, France (Gaul) plays the part of Pontius Pilate, the Roman procurator who complied with judicial murder and washed his hands of innocent blood; the crucifiers, of course, are Prussia, Russia and Austria, the evil nations that divided the spoils not unlike the Roman soldiers who cast lots for the garments of Jesus at the foot of his cross.* However, the crucifixion of the Polish nation at the time of the final partition, when revolutionary France failed to rescue its Polish ally, is conflated in the poet's mind with the immolation of 1831 when, so to speak, Poland was crucified afresh. So poignant and painful was the latter event to the defeated and despairing Poles that it awakened the romantic messianism of which Mickiewicz's poetic lament was the greatest but not the sole expression.[12] Another Polish poet of the same era, Kazimierz Brodzinski (1791–1835), invoked the same christological motif.

* John 19:23–24.

10

Hail, O Christ, Thou Lord of Men!
Poland, in Thy footsteps treading
Like Thee suffers, at Thy bidding;
Like Thee, too, shall rise again.[13]

Poland, like Christ, was a pure and innocent victim: however, unlike Christ, the Christ of Catholic faith – Mickiewicz was a zealous although highly unorthodox Catholic for whom Protestantism was anti-Polish as well as anti-papal – the Polish nation was not really or truly divine, in spite of its Christ-like character. The analogy in the final analysis was only an analogy; nevertheless, such was the poet's patriotic ardour that a spiritual fusion between Poland and Christ became almost more than a convenient poetic device. It verged on deification. In crucifying Poland, the contemporary "Satanic" emperors crucified freedom much as the ancient Romans had crucified a different but still related mode of freedom when they crucified Jesus of Nazareth. Once again the world was enslaved, both spiritually and politically, and once again the world was promised salvation. On the metaphorical 'third day,' the day of resurrection and revolution, the day when Polish freedom (i.e., independence) is finally restored, the poet believed, wars shall cease and a utopian age will dawn. It was commonly assumed by nineteenth-century democrats influenced by the French Revolution that only tyrants start wars; free peoples would never engage in war on their own volition. Polish freedom thus contained the promise and germ of universal freedom, the dissolution of all tyrannies and the inauguration of a new and blessed reign of God.

In this fashion, Mickiewicz envisaged a messianic age with Poland, like Israel of old, as its incandescent core. In this fashion, Poland, as the elect nation, became also the redeemer nation, the nation whose task it was to save a Europe "burning with the fires of despotism."[14] In this fashion, the redeemer nation became the Christ-nation or the Christ of the nations: "the nation on the rack, all anguish, all spirit, all idea, a pure principle."[15] In this fashion, the crucified nation was elevated to the realm of ideas, not just an idea but an Idea, as Norman Davies has written in his masterful history of Poland,[16] i.e., a consuming passion in the anguished minds of the Polish faithful, especially those who, like Mickiewicz, imagined themselves as the vanguard of the elect.[17] Among the émigrés, the latter was a lodestar, together with his fellow nationalist poets Zygmunt Krasinski and Juliusz Slowacki and the nationalist historian Joachim Lelewel, in spite of many differences in their political views. Polish messianism was not the creation of one man, but the fruit of an entire literary movement that flourished after the cruel martyrdom of

"Angel-Poland."[18] One man, however, Adam Mickiewicz, successfully placed the Polish Idea on Polish lips throughout the nineteenth and twentieth centuries, if not to the present day. While not everyone was converted to the poet's redemptive vision – many émigrés preferred less extravagant dreams and less eschatological solutions – the poetic *cri di coeur* could not be stifled by the police and censors of the alien regimes that had trampled and desecrated the sacred totem of Polish nationhood.[19] When a nation becomes an Idea, nationalism is in full flower.

Nationalism, as most students of the subject insist,[20] is more than simple patriotism, although super-patriotism invariably has nationalistic contours. Patriotism, the love of the *patria*, or one's country, is an ancient emotion, a natural instinct derived from feelings for hearth and home, and one of the virtues of the statesman from time immemorial. Nationalism, on the other hand, as we have seen, is a modern phenomenon, a novel and more complex form of patriotism that came into existence towards the end of the eighteenth century, although no single individual can be praised or blamed for its genesis.[21] It represents the birth of a new consciousness, a consciousness concerned with the collective identity and intangible unity of a single people, a consciousness that joins the patriot and his nation together in a sacramental union. "Now my soul is incarnate in my country," declares the hero in *Forefathers' Eve*, "My body has swallowed her soul, and I and my country are one." Although Poland, the enlightened commonwealth of old, the vast, populous, powerful and progressive state whose armies had once saved Europe from the Turks,★ was no more, Poland, the spiritual nation lodged in Polish hearts, was more real than ever to the dispossessed Poles, especially the educated elite. So also was its torture.

> I look at my unfortunate fatherland
> As a son at his father on the wrack,
> And I feel all the pain of my people
> Like a mother the child in her womb.[22]

Victimization is a powerful catalyst of political desires and agendas of every conceivable hue. The poets and writers of the age of exile freely employed sacrificial figures-of-speech because an old and pious Catholic society provided a fertile ground for images of suffering and expiation. Mickiewicz, Brodzinski, Krasinski, Slowacki and Lelewel drew from a popular well when they wrote of the crucified nation.[23]

★ At the Battle of Vienna in 1683 under King Jan III Sobieski.

Poland's 'Babylonian Captivity,' 'Sojourn in the Wilderness,' 'Descent into the Tomb,' 'Journey through Hell,' or 'Time on the Cross,' as it variously has been called,[24] inspired among the Poles something akin to the old Hebraic invocation: "If I forget thee, O Jerusalem!" or so one Polish historian declares.[25] The trauma of the tripartite partition was not the great defining moment in the evolution of Polish nationhood – in Polish historiography this honour belongs to the conversion of the Poles to Christianity in the tenth century[26] – but it transformed its nature. Henceforth a new and highly charged emotion saturated Polish literature, that "poetico-political dream world" into which the more literate Poles immersed themselves in their quest for solace amid the sorrows and tribulations of daily life, especially those subjected to Russian rule.[27] In their gifted hands the Polish nation became idealized and exalted as a thing of incomparable beauty and moral worth. Not only was Poland beautiful and virtuous, but also, according to Mickiewicz *et al.*, Poland alone was uniquely and profoundly Christian, indeed, the only real Christian nation in Europe because the Poles still worshipped the true Catholic God, whereas the other European nations, having succumbed to vulgar materialism, worshipped an assortment of idols. In no other country was Easter, the feast of the resurrection, celebrated with the solemn devotion found in the Polish churches, or so the nationalist poets claimed. The risen Christ and the risen nation were truly joined, psychologically and perhaps also metaphysically, in the believing mind. As the sacrificial death of a single man had saved individual human beings, the sacrificial death of a single nation will save all nations. As Christ was the elect man, so Poland was the elect nation in God's plan of salvation. As the martyrdom of Christ was a type or figure of the martyrdom of Poland, so in the eyes of faith the martyrdom of Poland completed the martyrdom of Christ.[28]

With these lofty sentiments, nationalism, true romantic nationalism, one of the distinguishing marks of the modern world, took root and blossomed in the Polish soul. In its Polish expression, Catholicism was the essential ingredient, the axis on which the idea of the Polish nation was made to turn, although, paradoxically, sixteenth-century Poland once had been a haven for persecuted Protestants and Jews: a tolerant realm in which freedom of conscience was allowed to flourish. This old generous mood, however, began to change as the counter-Reformation tightened its grip; nevertheless, during the romantic era, Polish nationalism was not given to narrow and exclusive definitions of what it meant to be a Pole, particularly those of an ethnic or racial character. The glorified Poland of the Polish poets, especially Mickiewicz, who actually grew up in

Lithuania,★ was still a diversified Poland, embracing different languages (not only Polish) and different sub-national minorities, despite the great writer's dislike of Protestantism. To be Polish had to do primarily with spiritual and political loyalties, with invisible rather than visible properties. A Pole was someone who felt himself to be a Pole: "gente Ruthenus, natione Polonus." Yet the nationalists who thus exalted the Poland of the spirit also promoted the veneration of the Polish language, preparing the way for a more linguistic and eventually more ethnic understanding of Polishness.[29] In due course, with the emergence of more intolerant political movements, a harsh and racially tinged nationalism scornful of romantic and religious values was destined to arise. Before this occurred, however, the cult of the Polish nation with its Catholic axis was modified by French and German ideas acquired abroad by expatriate Poles, wedding foreign influences to the native imagination.

Mickiewicz, for example, glorified Napoleon,[30] a dictator at home, indeed the first true modern dictator, but a liberator elsewhere, at least in the eyes of young European radicals who admired the French Revolution and hailed its torch of liberty, equality and fraternity. As a consequence, French idealism and French utopianism helped to mould his convictions, notably his vision of a golden age to come.[31] In his later writings, the poet conceived of a Polish messianic leader who would combine the spirit of Christ with the spirit of Napoleon, and, in pursuit of Poland's mission, lead a revolutionary crusade against the tyrannies of the age.[32] Europe would be saved by the sword, a view far from consistent with his much vaunted Christian beliefs, but Mickiewicz himself never bore arms and, like most romantics of his day, had little knowledge of the realities of war.

Other Polish literati as well, in fact the entire collective "flower of the Polish nation" and "knight-errants" of revolution, as they have been described,[33] managed to steep themselves in French culture and French political doctrines during the period of exile. Such was the prestige of France that even Poles of a conservative disposition – the émigrés were by no means of a single mind – turned to French theoreticians such as the anti-revolutionary Joseph de Maistre for arguments against political radicalism.[34] Among the more zealous pro-revolutionary Poles, notably the Paris-based Polish Democratic Society, on the other hand, the "Jacobin concept of the nation" made a huge impression.[35] This implied a nation of equal citizens in which all who dwelt on Polish soil, not only the privileged upper classes in the old 'democracy of the gentry,' were

★ The Grand Duchy of Lithuania was joined to Poland by the Treaty of Lublin in 1569.

accepted as part and parcel of the body politic, a departure from past Polish tradition with its strongly aristocratic predilections. The Jacobin concept appealed strongly to Lelewel, who, as a historian, idealized ancient Slavonic communalism. All the sons of Poland were one in the eyes of the French-inspired egalitarians and their Polish disciples. All the sons of Poland, however, were not one, if French counter-revolutionary doctrines were preferred. Krasinski, for example, a nationalist cut from far more conservative cloth than Lelewel, dreaded the prospect of a vast *jacquerie*★ in Poland should egalitarianism catch fire among the long disenfranchised and oppressed peasant masses, causing them to rise against their traditional masters: a fear cleverly exploited by the Hapsburgs in Galicia in 1846 in order to forestall a local insurrection led by Polish nobles against Austrian rule.[36] A national revolution was one thing; a social revolution with peasant freedom as its goal was quite another thing.

If France contributed much to the burgeoning of Polish national ideas and passions, so also did Germany. It was not unusual for Polish students to flock to German universities in order to sit at the feet of the illustrious figures of the German Enlightenment, an encounter that inspired a renaissance in Polish philosophy. Inevitably, the Polish philosophers also addressed the national question, sometimes in quite different terms than the romantic poets, seeing the latter as insufficiently critical as well as unduly emotional and unduly religious. On the other hand, a high degree of idealism and romanticism informed their own convictions, augmenting the intense patriotism of the era and the concomitant sense of Poland's special mission and destiny.[37] They too were nationalists. In contrast to the French Enlightenment, the German Enlightenment concentrated on the vitalistic as well as the rationalistic aspects of life, attaching metaphysical meaning to its hidden depths. Unlike France, a highly centralized state, Germany in the early nineteenth century was not unified politically, with the result that German nationhood was conceptualized by the Germans more in terms of language and culture than any form of political consolidation. Once Poland became effectively stateless after 1795, despite the Duchy of Warsaw and the Congress Kingdom, the French model no longer corresponded to the Polish situation, whereas the German model, although hardly stateless in the Polish sense, seemed to have more in common with a Poland divided into separate territories. Only stateless peoples, it has been claimed, are tempted to sanctify culture and language as national emblems, or, in the German case, a people burdened with too many states.[38] If no political basis exists for

---

★ From the fourteenth-century peasant uprising in France.

national unity, some other means of cohesion must be discovered and consecrated. As the nineteenth century advanced, Polish nationalism, more French than German in its inception, became more German than French in its evolution.[39] Certain German themes and obsessions found their way through Polish students into Polish thought where they were adapted with minor changes to fit Polish concerns. The German imprint on Polish thought is pronounced and unmistakeable.[40]

This imprint had to do with language as well as with speculative philosophy. Slavonic folklore cast the same spell on the Polish antiquarians as Germanic folklore had cast on the German antiquarians, men such as the eminent philosopher and man-of-letters Johann Gottfried Herder (Chapter III). Linguistic integrity cast a similar spell. Both Herder and his noted compatriot Johann Gottlieb Fichte (Chapter III) had emphasized its value to such a degree as to actually oppose French lessons for German children, even the cosmopolitan and universalistic Herder. Some nineteenth-century Polish intellectuals developed a similar fixation with the special properties of the Polish tongue, although others, less influenced by Herderian notions, refused to define their nationality in narrow linguistic terms.[41] Polish like German started to become the icon of a submerged and subjugated people, and, like German also, the mark of cultural and moral superiority. In fact, to one impressionable imitator of Germanic conceits, the purity of the Polish language served as proof of the "innate purity" of the Polish soul.[42] Even Fichte's extremely dubious concept of the *Urvolk* found its way into Polish nationalistic discourse.[43] This implied that the Poles were the true primordial people of Europe and that their speech was uncontaminated by extraneous elements, possessing an unspoiled and authentic quality that was denied the other bastardized European languages. Polish was seen as Europe's first, original and greatest tongue and the Slavonic Poles as Europe's first, original and greatest national and racial community. To think in this Fichtean manner was to assign Poland special status among the nations, much as the German philosopher assigned Germany special status in his 1807–8 *Addresses to the German Nation*★ (Chapter III). Not only French utopianism but also German metaphysics made their contribution to Polish messianism. While the Poles decided on their own that their country enjoyed the special protection of "God and his angels,"[44] there was nonetheless a Germanic flavour to the quasi-biblical belief adopted by the Polish nationalists that the exiled Poles, like the exiled children of Israel during the Babylonian Captivity, formed an

★ *Reden an die deutsche Nation.*

16

elect pilgrim community consigned with a special mission to save the world.[45] Clearly, the Polish students applied their German lessons well. Yet, in one important respect, the German model was alien to Poland. Protestantism, not Catholicism, was the religious axis of German nationalism.

As described above, the German philosophers left their mark on Polish minds, and indeed on other European societies as well. Like all national myths, the Polish idea had multiple origins; like all national myths also, it developed its own distinctive characteristics, for the configurations of Polish history were also distinctive, despite some parallels with other oppressed nations. Notions of election and special mission abound in modern nationalism, and, as we shall see, the concept of the Christ-nation is found outside of Poland,[46] but something unique still remains in the glowing ascriptions of the Polish poets and their political use of Catholic spirituality. Yet Polish thought was by no means uniform and the crucifixion theme was by no means the only leitmotif in Polish national discourse, even in the nineteenth century. Mickiewicz was actually castigated after his lifetime for abusing Christian symbols – to some Catholics, his use of Christ in his patriotic declamations was blasphemous – and for idealizing his country too much and thereby falsifying its entire historical record.[47] Poetry, it was argued by the nineteenth-century 'Warsaw positivists,' an anti-romantic faction dominated by Aleksander Swietochowski, represented a pernicious force in Polish politics, however melodic its lines and intoxicating its rhymes. The poetic strain in Polish nationalism was unhealthy and the national bards were false prophets as far as these exponents of harsh realism were concerned. Moreover old Poland with its social oligarchies was seen as largely responsible for its own downfall; state paralysis arising from an impotent central government and the notorious *liberum* veto★ as well as frequent civil discord had dragged the commonwealth to its doom. Whatever its true merits, the nation never was and never could have been as beatific or as Christ-like as Mickiewicz believed. To turn the Poland of the past into a kind of paradise lost was to endow it with virtues it had never possessed. As far as the new breed of realists was concerned, the poetic vision was essentially a lie.

Realism, however, seldom buoys the human spirit; romanticism

★ The ill-advised right of veto allowed every member of the national diet (Sejm). An invention of the fifteenth century, this constitutional measure was based on the notion that all Polish citizens (which did not mean all males in Poland) were both free and equal, thus effectively introducing chaos into the affairs of state. It was first used in 1652.

frequently has this effect. Hence the romantic dream was resilient, and continued to flourish, even if sporadically. The democracy of the gentry may have been responsible for Poland's demise, as the Warsaw positivists alleged, but, however defective, it was part of old Poland and its memory helped to preserve the sense of Polish nationhood during the long eclipse of the Polish state.[48] In particular, the widely admired democratic constitution of May 3, 1791, which Mickiewicz described as "carved from the hearts" of the Polish people,[49] served as an inspirational beacon long after the abolition of the Polish state and the abdication of the last Polish king.★ Its shining rays kept alive the hope of restoration, which in turn kept alive the spirit of rebellion throughout the nineteenth century. The 1830 uprising, after a fitful period, was followed by the 1848 uprising (against tsarist rule) as once again national aspirations were stirred. Poland was not the only cauldron of revolution during this second fateful year in European history, but the so called "Spring of Nations" failed to bring forth its anticipated resurrection and reunification.[50] Once again the forces of reaction were victorious. Their victory signified a temporary end to romantic messianic nationalism but not to nationalist passions *per se*. A new anti-romantic nationalist movement arose, born of disillusionment and therefore devoid of ethical idealism and religious zeal, but Mickiewicz and his romantic compatriots were not forgotten. Insurrectionist fires continued to blaze intermittently in the separated Polish lands until a third major anti-Russian uprising (the January Uprising) erupted in 1863 and a fourth in 1905, coinciding with the rise of mass politics in Europe with its ominous portents for the twentieth century. Further storms of repression raged; on the last occasion, however, the growing weakness of imperial Russia forced some concessions. Poland's time on the cross was not of short duration, although its torments were less onerous in Austrian-ruled Galicia where the Hapsburg monarchy permitted a much greater degree of local autonomy than was the case in the other Polish territories. Not all Poles, of course, clung to the dream of political and national rebirth, particularly in the Austrian realms; disheartened by constant defeat, many abandoned independence as a lost cause, favouring triple loyalty to the three imperial regimes instead.

Two men, Jozef Pilsudski and Roman Dmowski, both products of the changing ethos of the *fin-de-siècle* era, emerged as arch rivals in the renewed struggle for Polish freedom. Pilsudski was a soldier in the heroic mould and Dmowski an ideologue and, in the eyes of his enemies, a

---

★ King Stanislaw II August Poniatowski.

proto-fascist who founded a political party in his own likeness, the National Democrats. His ethnic and racially tinged nationalism was inspired by the fashionable Social Darwinist ideas of the day, and thus at variance with the idealistic religious nationalism of Mickiewicz and the romantic poets.[51] For one thing the National Democrats repudiated messianism as well as universalism, in other words, the treasured Polish great idea; for another thing they embraced antisemitism. National egoism defined their essence; "hatred, violence, oppression and exclusion," according to one hostile historian, defined their style.[52] Yet, in broad and general terms, Dmowski was no less an intellectual disciple of German ideas than the Polish idealists whom he despised. (There was a strain of antisemitism in Fichte.)[53] Fortune at last worked in favour of the Poles as a consequence of the general débâcle of the First World War. The Polish Second Republic was proclaimed in Warsaw in 1918 following the collapse of the Russian, German and Austrian empires. Like another soldier, Napoleon Bonaparte, much earlier in revolutionary France, Jozef Pilsudski in effect picked up power in the streets, and Polish independence was reborn in his hands, at least for a season. However, the Second Republic was troubled from its inauguration; war (with Russia), political assassination (of the Polish president), a violent military *coup d'état* instigated by Pilsudski himself (1926), dictatorship and finally economic collapse, robbed the Poles of the satisfaction that the sudden fulfilment of their national aspirations otherwise would have produced. When Hitler's legions swept across the Polish border in 1939, followed by a Russian invasion from the east, a new crucifixion was inflicted, a crucifixion far more terrible than all the oppressions of the past, a crucifixion in which Poland (to cite Norman Davies) was transformed literally into a Golgotha.[54]

The agony ended with the destruction of the German Third Reich in 1945, but a new captivity awaited the Polish nation. Stalin, the Soviet tyrant, victorious over Hitler, had no intention of granting the Poles any real freedom. Their liberation was ephemeral as civil conflict arose between communists and anti-communists with the former gaining the upper hand under Wladyslav Gomulka. The Polish government-in-exile in London was swept away and Soviet rule ensued under the supervision of the 'red tsar' in Moscow whose mind, in the words of one fawning Polish communist poet, was a "river of wisdom and reason."[55] Some Polish school teachers even instructed their pupils that Adam Mickiewicz himself had been a communist, although this ascription proved too much for other Poles, including even one communist president.[56] Accordingly the Republic of Poland was reconstituted in 1952 as the Polish People's

Republic – in effect, as a vassal state of a restored Russian empire in a communist totalitarian mould. This Poland, a dictatorship of the Polish United Workers' Party, bore no resemblance to the resurrected Poland envisaged by the romantic nationalists whose verse and prose had nurtured Polish dreams for generations. Nor, for that matter, did it resemble the Poland of the anti-romantic nationalists who had spurned messianism, or, indeed, the Poland of any other patriotic organization, although Gomulka in fact considered himself a patriot. Once again on the cross, the Polish nation, much reduced in geographical size, returned to a proxy form of its nineteenth-century subjugation.

The later subjugation, however, was destined not to last nearly as long as the previous one. Massive social and political unrest, coinciding with the general disintegration of the Soviet empire, finally caused communist rule to crumble in 1989, enabling the Poles to re-establish parliamentary democracy in the form of the Third Polish Republic. Lech Walesa, the labour unionist at the head of the main instrument of political transformation, the powerful Solidarity (*Solidarnosc*) movement, was the hero of the hour. As a symbolic gesture, the diet in Warsaw replaced the missing traditional crown on the head of the Polish national eagle, and the nation tasted something akin to the elation that accompanied the promulgation of the short-lived constitution of May 3, 1791 during which the king mingled with the people in the streets of Warsaw, incidentally losing his hat. The popular Walesa became president of Poland in 1990, but, to the surprise of the outside world, rapidly lost his popularity and therefore his presidency in 1995. Nevertheless a new order had arisen, accompanied by the restoration of Polish independence and autonomous statehood. The Russian shadow no longer fell with the same terrible menace over Polish soil. A Polish pope, John Paul II, in effect the uncrowned king of Poland, served to consolidate the Polish national image abroad.

Mickiewicz, one surmises, would have celebrated. The travail was no more, the third day had arrived, and the crucified nation had climbed out of its grave. True, no messianic age had arrived with Poland as its Mount Zion, but at least the Polish phoenix had arisen. After the better part of two centuries on the cross, that was miracle enough as far as those with reasonable expectations were concerned. The poetic fusion of Poland with Christ had served long as an article of faith for the romantic and religious nationalists, even if, as we have seen, many Poles had ceased to embrace this grandiose notion. Yet, however pretentious, Polish messianism, like all utopian dreams, was more than a fool's phantasmagoria. It supplied those who accepted its dictates with a deep and powerful motivation for clinging to their national identity under adverse conditions and thus from joining the roster of other lost nationalities. This was especially true during the worst periods, notably the Nazi era, when poetic themes of martyrdom and heroism were deliberately invoked to strengthen the national resolve.[57] It is well known that the simple recitation of familiar verses can enliven the human spirit in times of stress. To that degree, messianism probably saved Poland or at least contributed significantly to its salvation. However, as Poles themselves acknowledge, it also possessed a dark side, serving to promote self-righteousness as well as invidious contrasts through an excess of patriotism attended by xenophobia and insinuations of treason.[58] Mickiewicz himself was infected with these feelings: "Ye are not equally good, but he who is worse among you is better than the good stranger . . . "[59] Despite his universalism, the charismatic poet of the exile was by no means opposed to the shedding of alien blood if war was likely to advance the noble cause of political freedom. Those who regarded him with distaste had valid reasons for their antipathy. Xenophobia, however, was even more rampant among the latter-day enemies of the messianic tradition, especially Dmowski's National Democrats.

Today, in the twenty-first century, it is doubtful if many Poles seriously subscribe to the religiously inspired political visions of the old national bards, at least in their original form. In a less exalted but still idealistic fashion, however, the Polish idea – love of freedom, love of country, love of its Catholic ethos, love of chivalry, etc. – remains alive and efficacious, as does the legacy of Mickiewicz, whose name and 'divinely inspired words' are still revered in certain circles.[60] The Byronic hero was reburied in Poland in 1890.[61] Memories of past indignities and misfortunes still haunt the Polish mind, and, for good or ill or perhaps both, the great poet and his fellow romantics are still capable of stirring patriotic emotions in Polish hearts. Those who admire Mickiewicz have argued, rightly or wrongly, that romanticism helped to save the Polish people from worshipping the totalitarian state, as romanticism and totalitarianism are incompatible.[62] It has also been argued, rightly or wrongly, that without the romantic element in the national temperament the Solidarity movement of the Polish dissidents would never have arisen, for, like the nineteenth-century insurrections against the Russian tsars, the twentieth-century mass protest against the communist dictatorship was motivated by the poetic dream of freedom.[63] On the other hand, less admiring critics have decried the fact that, because of its tragic history, Poland, unlike most other nations, ended by nurturing a morbid "culture of defeat."[64] While failure reveals a profound truth about the antinomies of life – "the natural, inalienable fate of man"[65] – it also has undesirable effects if it leads to a dark obsession. As more than one cultural critic has pointed out, a romantic preoccupation with defeat and crucifixion can create a narcissistic "tragic posture" that is fraught with moral dangers.[66] Other examples of this sickness of the human spirit will emerge in later chapters in our study. In the meantime, one conclusion is certain. Whether healthy or unhealthy, the metaphor of the crucified nation cannot be relegated to the margins of modern politics: its potency endures, and, as we shall see, not only in Poland.

Notes

1 "The Books of the Polish Nation," *Poems by Adam Mickiewicz*, George Rapall Noyes (ed.), New York: Polish Institute of Arts and Sciences in America, 1944, pp. 376–377.

2 Abbé Henri Grégoire, cited in David A. Bell, *The Cult of the Nation in France: Inventing Nationalism 1680–1800*, Cambridge, Mass.: Harvard University Press, 2001, p. 15.

3 Michael Biddiss, *Father of Racist Ideology: The social and political thought of Count Gobineau*, London: Weidenfeld & Nicolson, 1970, p. 104.

4 Cf. Piotr S. Wandycz, *The Lands of Partitioned Poland, 1795–1918*, Seattle: University of Washington Press, 1974, p. 29.

5 Andrzej Walicki, *The Three Traditions in Polish Patriotism and their Contemporary Relevance*, Polish Studies Center, 1988, p. 10.

6 Fritz Stern, *Five Germanies I have Known*, New York: Farrar, Straus & Giroux, 2006, p. 383.

7 Andrzej Walicki, *The Enlightenment and the Birth of Modern Nationhood: Polish Political Thought from Noble Republicanism to Tadeusz Kosciuszko*, trans. Emma Harris, Indiana: University of Notre Dame Press, 1989, p. 7.

8 Ibid., p. 117.

9 "Forefathers' Eve, Part III," (Dziady) cited in *Poems by Adam Mickiewicz*, pp. 292–293. Mickiewicz, who was known as Poland's great national bard, was also the author of *Konrad Wallenrod* and *Pan Tadeusz*, both classics of Polish poetry and powerful expressions of his nationalist ideals.

10 See the essay by Jan Lechon in *Adam Mickiewicz: 1798–1855 Selected Poems*, Clark Mills (ed.), New York: Noonday Press, 1956, p. 43.

11 Roman Koropeckyj, *The Poetics of Revitalization*, New York: Columbia University Press, 2001, p. 1.

12 Andrzej Walicki, *Philosophy and Romantic Nationalism: the Case of Poland*, Oxford: Clarendon Press, 1982, p. 242.

13 Cited in Norman Davies, *God's Playground: A History of Poland*, Vol. II, New York: Columbia University Press, 1982, p. 9.

14 Walicki, op. cit., p. 117.

15 J. L. Talmon, *Political Messianism: The Romantic Phase*, London: Secker & Warburg, 1960.

16 See Davies, op. cit., p. 9

17 Koropeckyj, op. cit., p. 117.

18 Cf. Brian Porter, *When Nationalism Began to Hate: Imagining Modern Politics in Nineteenth-Century Poland*, New York: Oxford University Press, 2000, pp. 20–27. The term "Angel-Poland" comes from one of Krasinski's psalms.

19 Ibid., p. 245.

20 For example. Elie Kedourie, *Nationalism*, New York: Frederick A. Praeger, 1961, pp. 73–74.

21 Craig Calhoun, *Nationalism*, Minneapolis: University of Minnesota Press, 1997, p. 9.

22 From the translation by Louise Varese.

23 Cf. Joan S. Skurnowicz, *Romantic Nationalism and Liberalism: Joachim Lelewel and the Polish National Idea*, New York: Columbia University Press, 1981, p. 97.

24 Davies, op. cit., p. 18.

25 J. L.Talmon, *The Myth of the Nation and the Vision of Revolution: The Origins of Ideological Polarization in the Twentieth Century*, London: Secker & Warburg, 1981, p. 34.

26 Talmon, "Nationalism, Internationalism, World Pluralism," *The Jerusalem Colloquium on Religion, Peoplehood, Nation, and Land*, Marc H. Tanenbaum & R.J. Zwi Werblovsky (eds), Jerusalem: October 30–November 8, 1970, p. 246.

27 Davies, op. cit., p. 37.

28 Walicki, *Philosophy and Romantic Nationalism*, p. 249.

29 Ibid., p. 73.

30 Clark Mills (ed.), op. cit., p. 49.

31 Koropeckyi, op. cit., p. 100.

32 Andrzej Walicki, *Philosophy and Romantic Nationalism*, p. 263.

33 Talmon, *Political Messianism: The Romantic Phase*, p. 268.

34 Cf. Rett R. Ludwikowski, *Continuity and Change in Poland: Conservatism in Polish Political Thought*, Washington: Catholic University of America Press, 1991, p. 60.

35 Walicki, *The Enlightenment and the Birth of Modern Nationhood*, passim.

36 Talmon, op. cit., p. 267.

37 Cf., Walicki, *Philosophy and Romantic Nationalism*, Part II. It is interesting that the poets regarded the philosophers, most of whom were influenced by Hegel and Schelling, as too rationalistic and insufficiently religious. The major philosophical writers were August Cieszkowski, Bronislaw Trentowski, Karol Libelt, Henryk Kamienski and Edward Dembowski.

38 Ibid., p. 77.

39 Ibid., p. 89. "The gradual replacement of the political definition of nation by the ethno-linguistic conception was certainly one of the most important shifts in the Polish thought of the late Enlightenment."

40 Ibid.

41 Cf. Stanislaw Eile, *Literature and Nationalism in Partitioned Poland, 1795–1918*, Basingstoke: Palgrave Macmillan, 2000, pp. 13–14.

42 Ibid., p. 36.

43 Davies, op. cit., p. 28.

44 Elie, op. cit., p. 26.

45 Koropeckyj, op. cit., p. 111.

46 For example, in French political literature (Saint-Simonianism), which may in fact have influenced Mickiewicz. The theme was later taken up by Victor Hugo. See Walicki, *Philosophy and Romantic Nationalism*, p. 245.

47 Eile, op. cit., p. 134.

48 Walicki, *The Three Traditions*, p. 10.

49 Cited in Ludwikowski, op. cit., p. 43.

50 Wandycz, op. cit., Chapter 7.

51 Dmowski published his ideas in his popular book, *Mysli nowoczesnego Polaka* (Thoughts of a Modern Pole), 1902.

52 Porter, op. cit., p. 191.

53 As, for example, his suggestion in his commentary on the Fourth Gospel that Jesus was probably not a Jew since the evangelist failed to provide him with a Jewish genealogy.

54 Davies, op. cit., p. 80.

55 Adam Wazyk, cited in Richard Hiscocks, *Poland: Bridge for the Abyss? An Interpretation of Developments in Post-War Poland*, London: Oxford University Press, 1963, p. 146.

56 Ibid., p. 169.

57 Ibid., p. 190.

58 Eile, op. cit., p. 190f.

59 Cited by Walicki, *Philosophy and Romantic Nationalism*, p. 250.

60 Elie, op. cit., pp. 46–47.

61 Walicki, *The Three Traditions*, p. 16.

62 Ludwikowski, op. cit., p. 269.

63 Ibid., p. 271.

64 Maria Janion, cited in Walicki, *The Three Traditions*, p. 20.

65 Ibid.

66 Ibid., p. 22. (Stefan Kisielewski) In a memorable passage, the Protestant theologian Paul Tillich, writing between the two world wars, described modern man as tempted to dramatize his fate in aesthetic terms, contemplating himself "'Narcissus-like' as in a mirror in a self-destructive fashion" (Paul Tillich, *The Protestant Era*, trans. James Luther Adams (Chicago: University of Chicago Press, 1948, p. 204).

II

The Crucified Nation

FRANCE

In his savage polemic against Prince Louis Napoleon Bonaparte, *Napoleon the Little* (Napoléon-le-Petit), published in Brussels in 1852, the poet and novelist Victor Hugo (1802–1885) gave vent to his anger by imitating the Polish poets.

There was among the peoples one people which was a sort of eldest brother of the family of the oppressed, which was like a prophet in the tribune of mankind. This people took the initiative in all the movements of humanity. It said, "Come!" and all followed. As a complement to the fraternity of men which is in the Gospel, this nation taught the fraternity of nations. It spoke by the voice of its writers, of its poets, of its philosophers, and its orators as by a single mouth; and its words went to the extremities of the world, to settle like tongues on fire on the brows of all nations. It presided at the Divine Supper of human intelligence; it multiplied the bread of life of those who wandered in the desert. One day a storm encompassed it; it walked over the abyss and said to the frightened peoples, "Why fear ye?" The waves of the revolutions it raised grew calm under its feet, and far from engulfing, glorified it. Nations sick, suffering, and feeble pressed around it. This one limped; the chain of the Inquisition, riveted on her limbs for three hundred years, had lamed her: it said, "Walk!" and she walked. This other was blind; the old Roman papism had filled her eyes with fog and with night: it said to her, "See!" and she opened her eyes and saw . . . One day it approached dead Poland; it lifted its finger and cried, "Arise!" and dead Poland arose.

This people the men of the past, whose fall it prophesied, dreaded and hated. By craft, and tortuous patience and audacity, they seized and succeeded in garroting it at last. For more than three years the world has witnessed a gigantic execution, a frightful spectacle. For more than three years the men of the past, the scribes and pharisees, the publicans and the high-priests, are crucifying, in the presence of the human race, the Christ of the peoples, – the French people. Some have furnished the cross, others the nails, others the hammer. Falloux has placed on her brow the crown of thorns; Montalembert has pressed the sponge of gall and vinegar on her lips; Louis Bonaparte is the wretched soldier who has pierced her side and forced from her the last cry, "Eli! Eli! Lamma Sabacthani!"[1]

Hugo, like Mickiewicz, was a romantic nationalist whose imagination knew no bounds; like Mickiewicz also, he was a Catholic or at least of Catholic extraction, even if far from orthodox in his beliefs.[2] Consequently biblical images flowed freely from his pen, both in his prose and in his poetry. The poet-novelist was not only a nationalist; his nationalism, like his life, was coloured by his frequently changing moods and political allegiances. In his youth an ardent royalist – he received a literary reward for his Odes from King Louis XVIII, attended the coronation of King Charles X, and later frequented the soirées of King Louis Philippe – he became in his middle years a secular republican. His conversion to secularism and republicanism, however, was slow and fitful, consolidated only by his personal abhorrence of the prince-president of the Second Republic, soon to turn itself into the Second Empire. On the other hand, Victor Hugo's devotion to France itself was constant, and probably intensified by his eventual adoption of the civic ideals of the 1789 revolution as well as its promethean spirit. His France, like Mickiewicz's Poland, was a highly idealized France, a messianic France, a nation unlike other nations, a nation that in some profound sense was indubitably chosen, if not by God then by the mysterious workings of destiny. However, this 'truth,' which is religious in essence, was not devised by Hugo himself; it was revealed much earlier to Marguerite-Marie Alacoque, the seventeenth-century Visitationist nun who promoted public devotion to the Sacred Heart (Sacré-Coeur) of Jesus as a balm for the ills of France.[3] In later time the Sacred Heart became a potent symbol of the Catholic counter-revolution as well as an emblem of French favour with God.[4] Only a chosen nation can be anointed as a Christ-nation, and only a Christ-nation can play a redemptive role in the great drama of world history. Only a Christ-nation is certain to be crucified.

Who then crucified France, the Christ-nation or Christ of the Nations? The enemies of freedom crucified France, for France, at least to its republican children, was the incarnation of freedom and its apotheosis. These enemies are exemplified in Hugo's overwrought and partly mendacious 1852 tract about Comte Frédéric de Falloux, Comte Charles de Montalembert and especially about the prince-president himself. (Unlike the crucifiers of Poland, the crucifiers of France were internal rather than external, although they were soon replaced by external villains as French nationalism grew more shrill later in the century.) Falloux was the minister of education in the Second Republic, remembered mostly for the Loi Falloux of 1850 which gave the church effective control of public education throughout the country, whereas Montalembert played a major role in aligning Catholic support behind the head of state, about to ascend the throne as Napoleon III, emperor of the French. In Hugo's ex-Catholic eyes – his original Catholic convictions were forsaken with his original royalist convictions – clericalism and absolutism were the cardinal sins of these two agents of the emperor-to-be, although both men by the standards of the day were actually political liberals. They were nevertheless crucifiers of France, but the arch-villain and arch-crucifier was Louis Napoleon himself.

The prince-president, according to Hugo, violated his oath of office and sealed his violation with a massacre (December 4, 1851) that, again according to Hugo, resulted in rivers of blood streaming down the boulevards of the "sacred city," the "second Eternal City" of Paris. This much exaggerated Napoleonic 'whiff of grapeshot' was not merely the end of the republic and therefore the end of freedom, but also, in the writer's intemperate opinion, the virtual death of France itself. No crime was too great to be charged to the new autocrat, and it was no coincidence that Hugo, who published his book against Louis Napoleon in Brussels, was forced to spend the next eighteen years in exile on the British channel islands of Jersey and Guernsey waiting for the empire to crumble. Eventually his hopes were realized. After a twenty-year reign devoted to the self-enhancing politics of glory, Napoleon III lost his throne in 1870, following the Franco-Prussian War and the military disaster at Sedan, but the nation's time on the cross was by no means at an end. To Hugo's fury, a "Teutonic Caesar" – the King of Prussia or perhaps his chancellor Otto von Bismarck – and his armies threatened France with conquest, bombarding the second 'eternal city' of Paris with cannon fire before imposing a ruinous and humiliating peace that included the forfeiture of sacred territory, the provinces of Alsace and Lorraine.

O France! Will you perish? No, because if you were to die evil would live, fear would live; the window of dawn would be shut; one would see death born, the immeasurable death of all things. The extinction of Nineveh, of Tyre, of Athens, of Zion . . . would be nothing compared with your enormous eclipse, O France . . .

No, France. The Universe requires you to live.

You will live. The future would perish under your shroud.
France, France, without you the world would be alone.[5]

Tyrannical forces, the poet-novelist was convinced, were arrayed against France, the great bastion of republican liberty, but, regardless of its terrible sufferings, especially at German hands, his faith in its unique and chosen status remained intact. The Christ-nation would arise from its temporal death and overcome its enemies in a holy war (*revanchisme*) that would result in the restoration of its lost territories. Indeed, more than the lost provinces, it seems, for the "natural frontier" of Hugo's France extended to the left bank of the Rhine, a geopolitical notion entertained earlier by Louis XIV. The idea that nations possess natural frontiers, that is to say frontiers assigned by nature itself, became a standard feature of romantic nationalism in many lands. So inflamed was Hugo's messianic and militaristic zeal for the razing of old despotisms that something akin to the revolutionary enthusiasm of 1789 as well as its sequel in Napoleon I (not Napoleon III) has been ascribed to his writings and orations.[6] The poet-novelist never regarded the first emperor with the peculiar aversion that he bestowed on the last; for one thing, his father Léopold Hugo had been one of Napoleon the Great's generals, and, as a small boy, the future literary virtuoso had travelled to Italy and Spain with his family during his father's campaigns. Nurtured thus on military adventurism and French expansionism, he probably would not have objected to the enlargement of France had fortune favoured French rather than Prussian arms in 1870, despite his hatred of the latter-day Napoleon.

Victor Hugo's vainglory was by no means unique. His slightly older contemporary, the popular historian Jules Michelet (1798–1874), also transmuted Catholic pietism into a secular article of faith, believing also that France was a nation anointed by destiny to play a redemptive role in the forthcoming struggles of the oppressed and enslaved on every continent. "You live for the salvation of the world!," he told the French in his nationalistic tract *Le Peuple*, written during the reign of King Louis Philippe: "You are not only a nation but also a principle, a great political principle that must be preserved at any cost."[7] The political principle, not surprisingly, was embodied in the French Revolution, which Michelet, even more than Hugo an ardent republican, glorified and actually likened in an oblique and fanciful manner to the birth of Christ. The fateful year 1789 was deemed the central point in historical time, the great moment of revelation (along with, as we shall see, the life and death of Jeanne d'Arc) in French and therefore in universal history, the moment when the elect nation chose to die in order to rise again and extend its "immense, unbroken stream of light" throughout the heavens like a "veritable Milky Way."[8] If France ever came to grief, he prophesied, nothing less than a new glacial age would descend on the world:

> No doubt every great nation represents an idea important to the human race. But great God! How much more true is this of France! Suppose for a moment that she were eclipsed or had perished; the sympathetic bond of the world would be loosened, broken, and probably destroyed. Love, which is the life of the world, would be wounded in its most vital part. The earth would enter into an age of ice which other worlds have already entered.[9]

Michelet, whose emotional and thoroughly subjective history of France made its author famous, poured the same nationalistic passions into his highly glorified account of the tragic tale of Jeanne d'Arc, the 'Maid of Orleans' who saved the French Kingdom from the English invaders only to perish at the stake on May 30, 1431. Not only does his portrait of her trial and execution seem to echo the passion of Jesus in the gospels – the cruelty of the soldiers, the mob howling for blood, the forgiveness uttered by the dying martyr – but also the maid herself is transformed into a Christ-figure from whose death issues her nation's redemption. Michelet was scarcely alone in adopting this quasi-religious view. Jeanne d'Arc, declared the novelist Alexandré Dumas, no doubt swept away by the same patriotic excesses, is the "Christ of France . . . like Jesus, she suffered her passion; like Jesus, she had her Golgotha and her Calvary."[10] She was the Christ of France, she was also France itself, or at least its personification, since France, the Christ-nation, was martyred along with Jeanne and since France to men of this mental disposition was the instrument of the world's salvation. Michelet was quite explicit: a transcendental moral idealism pulsated in the French soul from Saint Louis to Jeanne d'Arc to the "young generals" of the 1789 revolution.[11] Even Napoleon, who had modelled his life on Alexander the Great, Caesar and Charlemagne, managed to become a Christ-figure in the eyes of his most fervent admirers, with St. Helena as his Golgotha.[12] Like the warrior-maid of the Middle Ages, the revered and larger-than-life Corsican man of genius personified France and was immolated as a consequence. Only a blind leap of faith could have produced such an unlikely metamorphosis, proving that the secular Enlightenment was no less prone to dogmatic claims than the old orthodoxies of church and state. In the case of Jeanne, even secular republicans could embrace a woman-saviour and female embodiment of the nation since her figure merged to some extent in their minds with that of Marianne, the allegorical representation of the revolution and its egalitarian credo: the red-capped woman of the people and emblem of the republic whose statue still adorns the town halls and public squares of much of France.[13]

Michelet himself abandoned Catholicism in a sudden "ideological" conversion during his tenure at the Collège de France where, incidentally, he rubbed shoulders with the exiled Polish patriot Adam Mickiewicz whose own Catholicism had taken a pronounced heterodox turn. Following his dramatic change-of-heart he lashed out against Christianity in almost Nietzschean terms as a "religion of slaves."[14] Henceforth the nation became his idol, meaning the French people rather than the French ruling classes, scornfully characterized as a "government of Jesuits allied with the government of king-bankers and banker-kings."[15] *Le Peuple* was written in an anti-clerical as well as a republican vein, for, as with Hugo, anti-clericalism and republicanism went hand in hand. No longer would its now controversial author tutor the daughter of the king, Princess Clémentine. France replaced Christ in the historian's personal pantheon; France, the French people, acquired christological significance in his new nationalistic religion. Jeanne d'Arc, of course, like Michelet himself, in his own words a "blade of grass between two cobblestones," was of humble origin and thus a true daughter of the people and a true voice of its incomparable collective genius. This romanticized picture was entirely out of joint with the disturbed and troubled state of nineteenth-century French society, but that did not matter. If the peasants, the imagined heart of the nation because of their proximity to the soil, were hostile and savage as a result of many physical and social deprivations, that also did not matter. The mystique of French peoplehood soared above and beyond every ill. "France is a person," he declared, France is not and never can be like other lesser nations.[16]

In particular, according to Michelet, France is not like England, that soulless, materialistic and egotistical rival to the north and the historian's special *bête noire*. On the contrary, the French spirit, the spirit of the people, of which Jeanne d'Arc and the 1789 revolution constituted an epiphany, was suffused with sublime love and altruism, nobility and grandeur, such as could have found expression only on French soil. Jeanne, of course, had been anti-English; consequently the true spirit of France is also anti-English, a theme that did not appear for the last time in the many twists and turns of subsequent French historiography. If one protested that the revolution had betrayed its ideals by turning to mass murder and devouring its own children as well as the children of its enemies (i.e., the notorious Vendée),★ the republican historian had a ready answer. The Robespierrian reign of terror, he insisted, had nothing to do with the people; it was an ugly aberration on the part of a few miscreants who did not represent the true French nation.[17] It was not intrinsic to the new age with its *novus ordo saeculorum*. The revolution itself was truly beautiful, a world-historical moment with a world-historical mission (the Hegelian terminology was not coincidental), a veritable Bethlehem event; those who opposed it and continue to oppose it place themselves on the wrong side of the gods of history. For what is history in any case but a everlasting duel between nature and humanity, matter and spirit, fate and freedom? Which of these principles find their deepest embodiment in the Jacobin spirit of revolutionary France is easy to discern.

With such assertions – one hesitates to say arguments – Michelet propagated republican nationalism. It is impossible not to detect a strain of German romanticism in his paeans, notably in his stress on the significance of language and culture, a theme at least partly adapted from Herder.[18] Also Herderian was the French historian's fascination with national characteristics as well as his romantic conviction that an inner spirit (*force vive*) animates the nation. Another sign of German influence is found in Michelet's admiration for the supposedly natural (i.e., instinctual) lives of the French peasantry in contrast to the unnatural lives of the urban proletarians and their bourgeois overlords. His idealism, moreover, like German idealism, was sullied by a persistent note of antisemitism: the Jew in his eyes was the prototype of the unnatural man. Michelet admired Germany as much as he detested England until the Franco-Prussian war and the German humiliation of France near the end of his life. From this shock he never recovered. However, his exaltation of Jeanne d'Arc proved decisive in the future evolution of French nationalism, both of the political left and the political right. Largely because of Michelet, the

---

★ A western section of France that took up arms in defence of the king only to be savagely repressed. Robespierre described the royalist rebels as an "impure race."

crucified nation – was not the bombardment of Paris and the amputation of the border provinces a real crucifixion? – found its most potent icon in a fifteenth-century woman who, in less troubled times, might have remained half-forgotten in the dim twilight of the late Middle Ages.

The cult of Jeanne d'Arc, popularized by a new generation of nationalistic writers, flourished in the xenophobic atmosphere of the Third Republic, the successor state to the Second Empire after Adolphe Thiers, the executive head of state following the abdication of the emperor, liquidated the Paris Commune. Memories of the Hundred Years' War were mingled with the new devastation and the Prussians were even described as descendants of the mediaeval English oppressors,[19] although the Britain of Queen Victoria and Prime Minister William Gladstone had adopted a neutral attitude in the latter conflict. As always happens in the wake of a national catastrophe, the French were bitterly divided among themselves, and their divisions deepened when Captain Alfred Dreyfus, a Jewish officer in the French army, was arrested and charged with treason in 1894. The effects of this famous scandal were immense, deepening every antipathy embedded in the national psyche and fragmenting the nation on a visceral level. In their struggle for the soul of France, both the pro-Dreyfus and anti-Dreyfus factions fell into furious recriminations; each side saw itself as the incarnation of the true France and claimed Jeanne d'Arc as its own. Each side, revolutionary and reactionary, clerical and anti-clerical, republican and monarchist, found a way of deploying the martyred warrior heroine as a symbol of its own aspirations and its own vision of the French nation, either an idealized model of political freedom or an idealized model of political order.

Behind the person of Jeanne and her martyrdom loomed the person of Christ and his crucifixion. Correspondingly each party saw itself as victimized, casting Dreyfus as either a Christ-figure or a Judas-figure in a new passion drama in which either "Truth, Justice and Humanity" was placed on the cross or "Army, Church and Nation:" in other words, the revolution versus the counter-revolution.[20] Dreyfus himself was a convenient pawn in this clash of conflicting values and so also in a sense was the long departed Jeanne. Nevertheless few nationalist movements ever coalesced around so pliable an image and powerful a cult as that of Jeanne d'Arc, one capable of drawing support from so many factions and shades of national opinion. Voltaire's old comic and iconoclastic poem *La Pucelle d'Orléans* (1762), which had once amused the French public, was no longer thought amusing after the Franco-Prussian war when the nation once again found itself ravaged and occupied by an alien army.

On the republican side, the poet and literary journalist Charles Péguy

(1873–1914), an ardent Dreyfusard, although curiously also an ardent Catholic, followed in Michelet's footsteps by promoting the myth of Jeanne d'Arc in the same hyper-nationalistic key.[21] Péguy's fascination with Jeanne arose both from his devotion to his nation and his devotion to the Catholic God, to whom he turned after tiring of the atheism of his youth. His Catholicism, however, was scarcely conventional, since he neither attended church nor arranged for his children to be baptized. It was mystical rather than clerical, and interwoven with republicanism as well as utopian socialism: indeed, he went so far as to declare that any attempt to overthrow the republic was also an attempt to dethrone the Christian God.[22] Most of his contemporaries thought the reverse. Jeanne, as far as the poet-mystic was concerned, while a woman of the Middle Ages, stood for the double virtues of Catholic piety and republican freedom: a synthesis that could have transpired only on the sacred soil of the sacred nation. She was French and, like Péguy himself, of the people; and the French people, whatever their sins, are forever the special objects of divine love:

> Our Frenchmen – They are my favourite witnesses.
>
> . . .
>
> Such are our Frenchmen, says God. They are not without their faults. Far from it.
> You might even say they have a great many faults.
> They have more faults than other people.
> But with all their faults I love them still more than I do all the others who, supposedly, have fewer faults.
> I love them as they are.
>
> . . .
>
> Now those Frenchmen, just as they are, are my best servants.
> They have been and always will be my best soldiers in the crusade.
> And there will always be a crusade.[23]

These lines were penned in 1912. True to Jeanne's zealous soul and heavenly mission to save her country from a foreign invader, in this case imperial Germany, Péguy died on the battlefield at Villeroy in 1914, a Christian martyr for God's favourite race.

On the anti-revolutionary side, another journalist with intellectual pretensions, Charles Maurras (1868–1952), drew opposite conclusions. A step-child of the Dreyfus affair and the literary pedagogue of the new ultra right organization Action Française, he also invoked Jeanne d'Arc as a symbol of France, albeit a quite different France from that of Péguy. The France adored by Maurras was nothing less than a "goddess" nation (*la déesse France*), a goddess, however, subject to fate in spite of her divinity, a goddess capable of perishing in the turmoil of the world unless her devotees see to her well-being by carefully tending her altars: "le culte de la patrie."[24] This meant, for Maurras, the restoration of the France in which the (recently canonized) Jeanne so passionately believed, the France of the old regime and the old monarchy, although, in fact, in his portrait of the desired king, the polemicist incorporated some thoroughly modern ingredients, notably the sinister leadership principle associated with Italian and German mass politics.[25] He also coined the modern term "integral nationalism," a concept that elevates the nation above the citizen as an end in itself: in other words, the defining principle of modern fascism. Maurras did not share Jeanne's religious faith; he was an agnostic, perhaps even an atheist, who treasured Roman Catholicism because of its Roman or Latin veneer, that is to say its classical character, because the aesthetic purity of classicism was essential to the French national genius. Nevertheless Jeanne's faith was fundamental for it sprang from the heart of France itself, from the real and true France (*pays réal*) of the pious mediaeval king St. Louis,★ another iconic figure, not the legal and false France (*pays légal*) that tolerated Jews, Protestants, Freemasons and other aliens. Furthermore, her piety – whatever one believes about her voices – saved her nation. Catholicism therefore was part of the national mould, an authoritarian hierarchical Catholicism, for Jeanne herself was no democrat, either religious or political, despite what the opponents of the Action Française may have thought. Maurras was quite explicit in this regard: "Cette héroïne de la Nation n'est pas l'héroïne de la Democratie."[26] Péguy was as wrong as wrong could be.

Jeanne d'Arc was not the only suffering woman in nineteenth-century French religiosity. Her female figure sometimes merged in nationalistic iconography with another highly revered female figure, the Virgin Mary, also a suffering woman who also became emblematic of France, the suffering nation. Mary, of course, was the mother of Jesus, who was crucified, and, in the flourishing Marian cults that sprang up on French soil as an apparent fruit of the spiritual and social disturbances of the age, she was easily associated with the redemptive vocation of her son. Popular piety was obsessed with suffering and suffused with themes of punishment and persecution, both in church and state.[27] Even social prophets of a secular bent found a peculiar appeal in the notion of redemption achieved through female pain: figuratively if not literally Mary was crucified as Christ was crucified![28] To the devout, the power of this image was

★ Louis IX (1226–1270).

immense, especially during sacrilegious and dangerous episodes such as the violent spasms of the Paris Commune when the Catholic archbishop of Paris and other clerics were murdered by angry mobs. The rage of the Communards was stirred by the close alliance between the altar and the throne during the Second Empire, an alliance that on a figurative level pitted the republican Marianne (by this time a virgin herself[29]) against the monarchist Virgin Mary! It was not without reason that the Third Republic was seen by Catholics as the scourge of the church. The immaculate Mother of God – the dogma of the Immaculate Conception had been promulgated in 1854 – not only suffered with her divine son but also with her beloved Catholic France, for which she had a special predilection not bestowed on other nations.[30] In this fusion of images, the suffering virgin (either Jeanne or Mary), the suffering Christ (depicted by the Sacred Heart), and the suffering nation formed a mystical union that many French patriots found compelling, particularly those with conservative sympathies. Anyone foolhardy enough to speak critically of the seraphic Jeanne, as a certain Sorbonne professor discovered in 1909, invited swift and violent retaliation. The efficacy still remains.

Despite the furious divisions between left and right bequeathed by the Dreyfus affair, Jeanne, the holy patriotic martyr, served to reunite her fractured country in the union sacrée proclaimed by President Raymond Poincaré in 1914 as France braced itself against another German invasion. Some impressionable clerics believed that General Joseph Joffre's success in halting the German army in the Battle of the Marne was nothing less than a miracle instigated by Jeanne herself.[31] Once again the French nation was in danger of crucifixion and once again in desperate need of symbols of redemption. Despite immense French and Allied losses, however, the long and terrible war to end all wars concluded with the defeat of imperial Germany and the recovery of Alsace and Lorraine. It now became Germany's turn to be crucified. While the French were victorious, their victory was pyrrhic since their casualties were the highest in Europe. France was utterly debilitated and never fully recovered from the financial and social devastation inflicted by the struggle, even if the national economy managed to expand until the Great Depression of 1929. Yet, in the midst of these continuing sorrows, or perhaps because of them, the transcendent power of Jeanne continued to assuage those who believed in her healing powers. Her canonization on May 16, 1920 served to magnify these magical attributes while greatly exciting nationalist feelings in the French populace. Once again a gifted poet, Paul Claudel, wrote a quasi-religious drama, in this case an oratorio *Jeanne au Bûcher* (Jeanne at the stake, 1938) in which her life and death are explicitly linked to the passion of Christ, an *imitatio Christi* so exact that the agents in her condemnation are cast as Judas and Caiaphas figures.[32]

Claudel was enchanted by Péguy's earlier exaltation of the beatified peasant girl of national lore. Her blood, like the blood of Christ, had expiatory significance for her country since her death at the stake, that "luminous, triumphant exhalation of flesh and smoke," was intended to breathe life and unity into the souls of the divided and broken French.[33] This consoling thought was not lost on the true believers among his contemporaries, although no union sacrée drew together the polarized segments of the nation as another crucifixion threatened in 1939 with the rise of a remilitarized and vengeful new German Reich. A new time on the cross began with the sudden collapse of the French army in the Ardennes. The Third Republic, unpopular in any case for various reasons with many of its citizens, fell as swiftly as the Second Empire in 1870, and, like most fallen regimes, was soon consigned to dust and ashes. So huge was the shock of the unexpected defeat and the débâcle that followed in its wake – a débâcle memorably depicted by the murdered Irène Némirovsky in her posthumous novel *Suite Française*[34] – that the French found themselves faced only with the most bitter and dismal of prospects. Forced to sue for peace, a hastily assembled new government headed by the aged marshal Henri-Philippe Pétain signed an armistice with Nazi Germany (June 22) as fear of another (perhaps communist) revolution swept the traumatized nation. Nature abhors a vacuum, and no one forgot that the Paris Commune had seized power in 1871 on the heels of another unexpected defeat also at German hands. France required a saviour. Who would save France?

The answer was at hand: Pétain himself, a hero of the First World War, the victor of Verdun, a "Frenchman without reproach" in the words of the then Archbishop of Paris,[35] a "leader who saved us from the abyss" in the words of another admirer,[36] a man around whom a myth was already woven, "le mythe Pétain." Immensely popular in 1940 (a fact often overlooked), Petain was supported by much of the French populace, at least for the moment. Not surprisingly, his hierarchical instincts were strongly endorsed by the nationalistic devotees of Jeanne d'Arc, including Maurras and the Action Française. Le pays réel, the France of the anti-Dreyfusards, the France of the Sacré-Coeur, the France of the white carnationists★ ('white France'), had found its king at last, and

---

★ A term derived from the infamous day (June 4, 1899) on which gentlemen with white carnations in their lapels publicly insulted Emile Loubet, President of France, at a racetrack (Auteuil). One aristocrat actually struck the hapless Loubet with his cane.

the monarchist theoretician, more royalist than the Orléanist pretender (the Count of Paris), called for blind submission to the new order.[37] To those who believed in divine intervention, another miracle seemed imminent. Once before, in the nation's hour of need, God had designated a tutelary saint to defend the French against a foreign invader; was history about to repeat itself?[38] It did not require too much ingenuity, given the dire circumstances of the hour, to link the old general to the young warrior-maid. Prayers were written or rewritten in his honour, and his name, like that of Jeanne, was glorified.[39] Despite the fact that Germany rather than England was responsible for the invasion, the old mediaeval foe was once again demonized, especially after the British destruction of the French naval fleet at Mers-el-Kebir (July 3–4) to prevent the warships from falling into German hands. Vichy France, the État Français established under Pétain's baton in the negotiated 'free' zone in the southern part of the country, even contemplated joining the Germans in their projected invasion of England. Pierre Laval, Pétain's prime minister, was willing to supply Hitler with two hundred French pilots for this purpose.[40]

No invasion, however, was launched, and no miracle rescued the French from the lion's den. The anointed saviour turned out to have feet of clay and the mystique associated with his name was soon defiled by the moral squalor of his 'National Revolution,' especially as contained in Vichy's racial laws and the zeal demonstrated by the collaborationists in the seizure and deportation of the Jews, many of whom were French citizens and many of whom had sought haven on French soil from elsewhere in Europe. For this infamy, the État Français stands forever condemned, although the perpetrators were tried and convicted on other grounds after the liberation; no one wished to acknowledge the role played by French nationals in the true crucifixion of the twentieth century. To this day the subject remains controversial and painful. Pétain himself, like Laval, was sentenced to death; only the memory of Verdun and the intervention of Charles de Gaulle, the head of the provisional government (as well as another fervent nationalist in the mode of Jeanne d'Arc),★ saved him from Laval's fate. Nevertheless his final years in quasi-exile on an island near Brittany were lonely and ignominious, a cruel punishment for a once idolized hero. He died in 1951. Because an element of ambiguity has always encircled his motives, his death was followed by a partial resuscitation of his iconic persona, enhanced now with the aura of martyrdom.[41]

★ The cross of Lorraine, the home province of Jeanne, was chosen as a symbol of his political movement.

Pétain, like Jeanne, had personified France, and, like the nation itself, had suffered as a consequence, at least for those – a minority – who never lost faith in his greatness. In one form or another, Pétainism continues to haunt the national consciousness.

The most palpable form in which the same complex of ideas and passions has reappeared in more recent times bears the name of Lepenianism (*lepenisme*), meaning the social and political discourse of Jean-Marie Le Pen, the current leader of the Front National and a perennial candidate for the French presidency. This ultra right movement, in some measure the heir of the Action Française and integral nationalism, represents a fusion of various currents and factions on the margins of the political spectrum, some old and some new.[42] Its burning *raison d'être*, as delineated by Le Pen himself, is the defence of the nation – "une reaction de santé" – against the mortal perils posed by moral decadence, political subversion and alien invasion.[43] Since the recovery of national health is the great leitmotif of the Front National, and since health entails a knowledge of biology, Le Pen describes his crusade as 'biopolitical' rather than merely political.[44] Thus he adorns integral nationalism with a more scientific façade. Since biology matters, indeed, matters above all else, the triple dangers are generally rendered in biological (i.e., racial) terms, borrowing extensively from the scientific and pseudo-scientific language made fashionable by a new generation of Social Darwinists, especially the language of that peculiar mix of sociology and the life sciences that calls itself sociobiology. Homogeneity is healthy, heterogeneity unhealthy, in the nation; consequently racial admixture is to be abhorred lest a morally debased society arise, a society afflicted with what one exponent of national purity in post-colonial France has described as the horrors of 'caféaulaitisation' (coffee-and-milk discoloration).[45]

This cult has attracted its own intelligentsia. In Le Pen and his racialist entourage one hears a distinct echo of the distant voice of Count Arthur de Gobineau, the nineteenth-century author of a long melancholy treatise on the decline and fall of civilization[46] and a man for whom Paris was a racial cesspool, an abyss over which French culture was suspended and into which it was doomed to sink. Despite its scientific veneer, Lepenian philosophical jargon clearly reflects the xenophobia of disgruntled elements in the nation unable to transcend the bitterness of defeat and troubled by the loss of empire and the loss of national prestige. Antiimmigrant (especially anti-Arab), antisemitic – Le Pen has dabbled in various covert ways of maligning Jews (and Masons) without violating the letter of French law,[47] including historical revisionism★ – anti-egali-

---

★ Denial of the holocaust.

tarian, authoritarian if not totalitarian, the Front National has made itself the voice of militant nationalism in contemporary France. Significantly, in spite of Le Pen's biological determinism, a religious component has attached itself to his ideas, invoking old Catholic values in what was once a church dominated social order and in what still remains, at least *pro forma*, a largely Catholic country. "Dieu, Famille, Patrie" has become a political slogan in company with "la France aux Français!," conveying more or less the same meaning.[48] Exemplified once again is the ease with which nationalistic language so readily mimics religious language, appropriating for its own uses the concepts, symbols and icons of the religion most closely identified with the national culture and history. In the French case, this meant the God in whose name the Frankish king Clovis was baptized in 496; it also meant the cult of Jeanne d'Arc.

It is only natural, therefore, for Le Pen and his party to invoke the legend of the martyred warrior-maid. The leader himself, side by side with other representatives of traditionalist France, "la France des cathé-drales," marched in procession on the feast-day of the female Catholic saint in May, 1981: a highly charged public statement with political as well as religious overtones. His public action animated old ghosts: Péguy and Maurras, of course, but also Maurice Barrès (1862–1923), another devotee of Jeanne d'Arc and another nationalistic revivalist famous for his authoritarian views and his doctrine of the earth and the dead ("la terre et les morts"). In 1898 Barrès had helped to found the League of the French Fatherland (Ligue de la Patrie Française) in opposition to the League of the Rights of Man. In his ears rang the Song of Roland (La Chanson de Roland), invoking the heroic eighth-century death at Roncevaux at Saracen hands of still another national icon. To be French, according to Barrès, means to possess psychic roots in the French earth and the French past, and to draw spiritual sustenance from the French dead, the ancestors and progenitors of the nation.[49] Le Pen would not disagree; the Song of Roland rings also in his ears. France is always paramount, and only the true French, that is to say, only those with French parents who have been nurtured on French soil and steeped in French culture and French history, only those who truly love Jeanne d'Arc, belong to France; all others are merely resident aliens. Because France is paramount, French heroes are also paramount, Jeanne herself is paramount, a patriotic and Christian demi-goddess whose numinous power extends beyond the borders of France to other European nations. Although a child of the fifteenth century, she and the nation that she personifies constitute a perfect moral ideal to be emulated by the modern world. Jeanne and France stand on a pedestal together, a shining inspiration to all. When asked in an interview what role model he would select for the European youth of today, Le Pen replied as follows:

> As paradoxical as it may seem for a man, my great European is a woman: Jeanne d'Arc. In this national heroine, patriot and saint as well as champion of Christianity, one discovers youth, the common people, faith and sacrifice, all the components of civilization. Jeanne d'Arc was an inspired shepherdess who became commander-in-chief and died before the age of twenty at the stake, a victim of ingratitude and injustice, which probably constituted the gates of heaven for her. Her greatness of spirit, her perseverance in pursuit of her goal and the profound significance of her national deeds are so many examples for the French and the Europeans of today . . .
>
> . . .
>
> What, in fact, is so unique in the person of Jeanne d'Arc is that she dedicated her life to serving her king (or her country) and serving Christendom (or the Europe of her day) at one and the same time, and on top of all that serving God. Jeanne d'Arc attained a perfect equilibrium, an admirable synthesis of love of her people, love of her nation, love of her king, love of Europe and love of God. In this she was a complete heroine . . . She is the foremost and most complete symbol of France as she is also that of Europe.[50]

France is Jeanne, Jeanne is France: the crucified nation awaiting its resurrection. How Catholic the French cult of the nation has remained! – Catholic obviously for the children of the counter-revolution but Catholic even for the secular children of the revolution, in spite of their periodic anti-clerical and even anti-Christian explosions beginning with Robespierre's bizarre Cult of Reason. The republicans, some historians have argued, simply transferred the notion of a sacral community, the *corpus Christi mysticum*, from the church to the nation, defining the latter in the words of a 1792 petition to the Legislative Assembly as "the sole divinity it is permissible to worship."[51] Hence republicans also could revere Jeanne d'Arc in spite of her monarchism, as we have seen with Péguy. National symbols, once they have become enshrined in the national consciousness and infused with sacred meaning, are not easily demolished, nor for that matter is religion itself. So powerful is the religious mould that Dominique de Villepin, prime minister of France (2005–2007), cannot refrain from describing the Battle of Waterloo (1815) in his large book about Napoleon as of all things a French crucifixion![52] Strange as this ascription seems, it is not without reason if one follows the logic of that school of thought that regards Napoleon as a "hero of democracy" and a "friend and liberator" of the nations, making Waterloo a "cruel destruction of universal liberation, the crucifixion of a redeemer, a new . . . Calvary."[53] As we have seen, some older republican nationalists also held the same remarkable opinion. Roland, Jeanne, Napoleon have been woven into the same seamless robe, but Jeanne is ascendant.

Notes

1 *Works of Victor Hugo*, Vol. VIII (trans.) Boston: Frederick J. Quinby, n.d., pp. 211–212.

2 For example, he was sufficiently anti-clerical to refuse the last rites of the church from the hands of the Archbishop of Paris when on his death-bed.

3 Cf. Raymond Jonas, *France and the Cult of the Sacred Heart: An Epic Tale for Modern Times*, Berkeley: University of California Press, 2000, p. 2.

4 Formed in opposition to the revolution, the Society of the Sacred Heart saw itself as the instrument of national salvation, especially during the savage civil war following the defeat of 1870 and the collapse of the Second Empire. Devout Catholics promised to build a great church dedicated to the Sacré-Coeur if the city was spared German occupation. The promise was fulfilled (Montmartre) during the Third Republic.

5 "L'Élégie des Fleaux," from *La Legende des Siècles*. My translation.

6 Cf. Graham Robb, *Victor Hugo*, New York: W.W. Norton & Co., 1997, p. 460.

7 *The People* (1845), trans. John P. McKay, Urbana: University of Illinois Press, 1973, p. 35.

8 Ibid., p. 193.

9 Ibid., p. 183.

10 In his paean *Jeanne d'Arc (1429–1431)*, (1842). Cited in Marina Warner, *Joan of Arc: The Image of Female Heroism*, Berkeley: University of California Press, 1981, p. 268.

11 Michelet, op. cit., p. 191.

12 Jules Michelet, *Joan of Arc*, trans. Albert Guerard, Ann Arbor: University of Michigan Press, 1967, p. xii, fn. 5. Emil Ludwig, in his famous and highly subjective biography of Napoleon (*Napoleon*, 1926) portrays the fallen emperor as a cruelly persecuted figure and a man far more noble than his captors in every conceivable way. Ludwig does not use the term, but an aura of crucifixion surrounds his account.

13 Cf. Maurice Agulhon, *Marianne into battle: Republican imagery and symbolism in France, 1789–1880*, trans. Janet Lloyd, Cambridge: Cambridge University Press, 1981, passim. However a tension lies between Marianne and Jeanne d'Arc: the former personifies the republic whereas the latter personifies the nation. The republicans, of course, made no distinction between the republic and the nation.

14 *Mother Death: The Journal of Jules Michelet 1815–1850*, Edward K. Kaplan (ed.), Amherst: University of Massachusetts Press, 1984, pp. 164, 177.

15 Ibid.

16 Cited in Stephen A. Kippur, *Jules Michelet: A Study of Mind and Sensibility*, Albany: State University of New York Press, 1981, p. 72.

17 Ibid., p. 165.

18 Michelet's friend Edgar Quinet translated Herder's *Ideen* into French.

19 Warner, op. cit., p. 238.

20 Christopher E. Forth, "Bodies of Christ: Gender, Jewishness and Religious Imagery in the Dreyfus Affair," *History Workshop Journal* (No. 48/Autumn 1999), p. 18.

21 Notably in his two most admired works, *Le Mystère de la Charité de Jeanne d'Arc* and *Les Tapisseries de Ste Geneviève et Jeanne d'Arc*.

22 Cf. *Le monde moderne*.

23 "Dieu et la France," (trans. Anne and Julian Green), *Charles Péguy: Basic Verities*, New York: Pantheon Books, 1943, pp. 235–236.

24 Charles Maurras, *Enquête sur la Monarchie*, Paris: Nouvelle Librarie Nationale, 1924, p. 474. It is noteworthy that the Comte de Paris, the pretender to the French throne, disliked and disapproved of the form of monarchism expounded by Maurras, seeing it as Caesarist and dangerous.

25 Cf. Ernst Nolte, *Three Faces of Fascism: Action Française, Italian Fascism, National Socialism*, trans. Leila Vennewitz, New York: Mentor Books, 1969, p. 153.

26 Charles Maurras, *Jeanne d'Arc, Louis XIV, Napoleon*, Paris: Ernest Flammarion, 1937, pp. 28–29.

27 Cf. Thomas Kselman, *Miracles and Prophecies in Nineteenth Century France*, New Brunswick: Rutgers University Press, 1983, p. 121.

28 Cf. Eugen Weber, *My France: Politics, Culture, Myth*, Cambridge, Mass.: Harvard University Press, 1991, p. 106.

29 Agulhon, op. cit., pp. 128–129.

30 Kselman, op. cit., p. 100.

31 Cf. Thomas Kselman, "France: Religion and French Identity: the Origins of the Union Sacrée," *Many Are Chosen*, William R. Hutchison & Hartmut Lehmann (eds), Minneapolis: Fortress Press, 1994, p. 66.

32 See Moya Laverty, "*Jeanne d'Arc au bûcher* and its place in the work of Claudel," Claudel: A Reappraisal, Richard Griffiths (editor), Chester Springs, Pa: Dufour Editions, 1968, p. 63f. The music in the oratorio was composed by Artur Honegger.

33 Warner, op. cit., p. 170.

34 A long lost work written in hiding by a Jewish woman novelist to be discovered and published over fifty years later.

35 Cited in James F. McMillan, *Twentieth Century France: Politics and Society 1898–1991*, London: Edward Arnold, 1985, p. 136.

36 Jean Berthelot, cited in Robert O. Paxton, *Vichy France: Old Guard and New Order 1940–1944*, New York: Columbia University Press, 1972, p. 14.

37 Cf. Ernst Nolte, *Three Faces of Fascism: Action Française, Italian Fascism, National Socialism*, trans. Leila Vennewitz, New York: New American Library, 1969, p. 115.

38 Ibid.

39 Cf. Nicholas Atkin, *Pétain*, London: Longman 1998, p. 109.

40 Ibid., pp. 66–67.

41 Ibid., p. 197.

42 Cf. Jean-Yves Camus, "Origine et formation du Front National (1972–1981)," *Le Front National à Decouvert*, Nonna Mayer & Pascal Perrineau (eds), Paris: Presses de la Fondation National des Sciences Politiques, 1989, pp. 17–22.

43 Jean-Marie Le Pen, *L'Espoir*, Paris: Editions Albatros, 1989, p. 108.

44 Ibid.

45 This term appears in an anti-egalitarian work popular among right wing intellectuals attracted to the politics of the Front National. See Henry de Lesquen et le Club de l'Horloge, *La Politique du Vivant*, Paris: Albin Michel, 1979, p. 151.

46 *Essai sur l'inégalité des races humaines*, 1853–55.

47 Cf., Maryse Souchard, Stephane Wahnich, Isabelle Cuminal, Virginie Wathier, *Le Pen: Les mots* (Analyse d'un discours d'extreme-droite), Paris: Le Monde Editions, 1997, p. 68.

48 Cf. Pierre-Andre Taguieff, "La métaphysique de Jean-Marie le Pen," Mayer & Perrineau, op. cit., pp. 187–189, fn. 2.

49 Maurice Barrès, *Scenes et doctrines du nationalisme*, Paris: Editions du Trident, 1987.

50 Jean-Marie Le Pen, op. cit., pp. 154–155. My translation.

51 Cited in David A. Bell, *The Cult of the Nation in France: Inventing Nationalism 1680–1800*, Cambridge, Mass.: Harvard University Press, 2001, p. 38. Bell maintains that French nationalism retained a Catholic substructure in contrast to its British Protestant counterpart.

52 Dominique de Villepin, *Les Cent-Jours ou l'esprit de sacrifice*, Paris: Librairie Académique Perrin, 2001, p. 424f.

53 Hans Kohn, *Prophets and Peoples: Studies in Nineteenth Century Nationalism*, London: Collier-Macmillan,1946, pp. 51–52.

III

The Crucified Nation
GERMANY

> Jesus was alone at that time (Gethsemane), as now the German people are
> alone, surrounded by the overflowing hatred of their enemies. This war
> is the Gethsemane of the German people.[1]

This poignant sentiment, expressed in a military sermon preached in
1917, was not uncommon among patriotic Germans during the tribulations of the Great War. Some Germans, such as the poet Kurt Heynicke,
resisted the temptation to cast their nation in the role of a betrayed and
abandoned Jesus, preferring to see all mortals in his image,* but many
chose otherwise, especially those who cherished the numinous union of
altar and throne. Such was the fervour of the pious patriots generated by
the clash of titans on the battlefield that comparisons between the
suffering nation and the suffering saviour came readily to their lips. "Our
German people (*Volk*) in this war are a favoured martyr people, a chosen
instrument in the hands of God. To be a German is to be obligated now
and for a long time to come to walk a solitary path among the nations.
But on this *via dolorosa* (*Passionwege*) roses . . . will blossom for us" – so

---

★ GETHSEMANE

All men are Christ.
In the dark Garden we must drink the cup
Father, let it not pass from us.
We are all of one love.
We are all deep pain.
All seek to be redeemed.
Father, Thy world is our cross.
Let it not pass from us.

declared another pastor, swept away by facile christological analogies.[2] "Yes, we Germans bear in these days something of the cross of Christ," declared a third ecclesiastic presumably from his Lutheran pulpit, adding that in the everlasting battle between good and evil, the good is often crucified because evil hates that which is good. This maxim was easily applied to the German situation where the good and the great (meaning, of course, the Germans) were enduring persecution at the hands of the mean and the small (meaning, of course, the apostate powers arrayed against Germany) that were obviously jealous of Germanic superiority (*Überlegenheit*). Do we hear in this statement a hint of the master race? Conceivably, for it was a period when race-thinking was popular and racial and religious terms were interchangeable and frequently intermingled. One thing at any rate was regarded as certain by the devout subjects of the Kaiser: in the current British, French and Russian assault on the German Reich, "Jesus was being crucified again." However, like the sacrifice of Christ two thousand years in the past, the German sacrifice in the present was not in vain, but a veritable a font of grace for Europe as well as for the entire world.[3]

To make the religious analogy as explicit as possible, the crucifiers of Christ-Germany were portrayed in New Testament images, either as Jewish mobs – invariably the superstitious masses of modern Russia (incidentally, an antisemitic ascription); or as self-righteous Pharisees – invariably the hypocritical modern English; or as mocking unbelieving Sadducees – invariably the sceptical and frivolous modern French.[4] Encircled by such nefarious time-honoured enemies, the devout German Christians found solace in their faith, or at least in a highly nationalistic rendition of its precepts and symbols. Without detecting anything offensive or wrong in their ideological use of scripture, they exploited its dramatic elements in order to serve their own political and military ends, confusing the God of Christianity with the tribal gods of hearth and home. "For Germany the way of the cross of Christ is the way of war, a passion to be followed by a glorious resurrection . . . a greater fatherland!" – so proclaimed still another patriotic enthusiast.[5] That this view of things, offensive to most modern ears, was not offensive when it was uttered in 1915, says much about the tenor of the times. With similar aplomb, a substantial part of the nation indulged in the most inordinate of emotions, elevating the national cause to an exalted spiritual plane. Not all Germans, of course – one thinks, for example, of the Spartacist (communist) leader Rosa Luxembourg – but enough Germans, especially in the state-related Protestant churches, fell into this form of nationalist monomania to lend a holy aura to the battle between Germany and its apostate foes, seen as the embodiment of the spirit of darkness (*Geist der Finsternis*) and evil.

The holy aura was luminous and its rays widely dispersed. Some zealous evangelicals found in the great national enterprise a God-given opportunity to win back the masses lost to the churches during the social dislocations of the industrial era, re-baptizing as it were the homeland of the Reformation.[6] Some German poet-dramatists also saw fit to pour their love for their country into suitable verse,★ although no German Adam Mickiewicz has ever been canonized, unless Arndt and Wagner in the nineteenth century are regarded in this light (see later). Some scientists also, as Albert Einstein observed to his disgust, were no less fervent in their religious nationalism than the patriotic churchmen, extolling the war in religious terms as a "path to purification and salvation," a test of faith imposed by God.[7] The enemies of Germany, including Russian, French and British Christians, were also inclined to enlist the universe on their side, although in the British case without the 'suffering messianism' characteristic of some other European nationalisms.[8] However, it is never a long or difficult step to the crucified nation motif in any country saturated with Christian symbols that regards itself as unfairly victimized. Catholic Poland, Catholic (even if secular) France and Protestant Germany were all susceptible, although obviously not with equal justification.

The Germans, according to Sir Isaiah Berlin, were the first true nationalists.[9] Much evidence supports this assertion, even if no single individual, German or non-German, can be designated the author of European nationalism. While the French Revolution was the great formative event that changed the face of Europe, churning new ideas and new passions in its wake, it was on German soil that nationalism became cultural and linguistic as well as civic and political, and it was on German soil that nationalism started to acquire a pronounced ethnic and racial cast. These traits are evident in the writings of many eminent Germans, notably the philosophers Johann Gottfried Herder (1744–1803) and Johann Gottlieb Fichte (1762–1814), the poet Ernst Moritz Arndt (1769–1860), and the Protestant theologian Friedrich Schleiermacher (1768–1834), all major figures in the German Enlightenment. In Germany as elsewhere, nationalist ideas sprouted first among men of letters, spreading later among the masses. These ideas did not arise in an intellectual void; an assortment of proto-nationalist writings predated the modern era.[10] One xenophobic work in particular, the late mediaeval

---

★ As an example, see Gerhart Hauptmann's poem "O Mein Vaterland."

Book of a Hundred Chapters, has even been described as a prologue to twentieth-century National Socialism.[11] Although some of the early texts are suggestive of things to come, extolling the German language and German identity in crude and chauvinistic terms, they do not constitute a body of nationalist literature except in an embryonic sense. Only with the dawn of a later age does the concept of the nation emerge in its full and unadulterated character as an *idée fixe*.

Nationalism, as we have seen, represents the birth of a new consciousness, a state of mind preoccupied with the mystique of collective selfhood. As part of the romantic *Zeitgeist*, a fascination with language and thus with folklore and literature dominated the intellectual landscape. The German literati regarded language as an index of nationality and a medium of the peculiar genius of each distinctive people. Language was highly instrumental in the stirring of national feelings because without a common tongue a sense of common identity is difficult to forge. Even the French Republic was forced to impose the French language throughout its regions on a score of sub-nationalities with different tongues and dialects. In Germany, however, a 'nation' divided into a score of kingdoms, duchies and city-states – some thirty-nine sovereign powers in 1815 – linguistic unity assumed a critical significance. No small part was played in moulding the new man of the new age (the nationalist) by literary revivals, often beginning with the study of tales and legends from the folkloric past, the relics of old Germany. Poets, dramatists, storytellers, artists and scholars contributed their manifold talents, most famously the Grimm bothers Jakob Ludwig Karl (1785–1863) and Wilhelm Karl (1786–1859) whose fairy tales are still widely read. As languages differ, so also peoples differ, and their differences fill the earth with diversity and lend it colour and splendour. The world is not monochrome. Each nation possesses a distinctive nature, a fact already known to the Age of Reason with its zeal for the classification of data, including human data. No nation is a mere aggregate of individuals; to the romantic mind, the nation instead is a type of individual-writ-large, a "corporate personality," as Hans Kohn writes, "endowed with common thoughts, sentiments and purposes."[12]

This notion, which destroys true individuality, acquired certain religious connotations. To the fathers of German nationalism and their imitators abroad, each nation and each national language is the cultural voice of the inner life spirit, that "great creative Kraft"[13] or invisible supernatural force that animates the peoples of the earth and their collective souls. Language arises from life and life arises from nature and nature is grounded in spirit (or Spirit), which means in God. Hence a transcendental meaning is attached to human diversity. Nature (i.e., God), the "steward of the world," loves each individual nation in its individuality, and, not wishing the nations to merge with or oppress each other, has supplied them with a wealth of contrasts as a "dam against foreign inundations." So at any rate Herder declared.[14] Since the nation rather than the state is the object of God's love, its creative and holy power is indestructible, even eternal. Political states like the old Polish commonwealth may perish, but, as an article of romantic faith, the Polish nation cannot perish. This we have seen in Chapter I.

Herder, despite his fondness for heterogeneity, was a cosmopolitan who repudiated all notions of special election; God has no favourite people, no *Favoritvolk*. Fichte, while also a cosmopolitan, believed otherwise. Initially, like many other young intellectuals and writers of the day, an ardent admirer of the egalitarian ideals of the French Revolution, he turned against the French when Napoleon invaded the German territories, including the Kingdom of Prussia. His anger found graphic expression in his famous speeches to the German nation (*Reden an die deutsche Nation)*, a series of public lectures delivered in French-occupied Berlin in 1807–8 in defiance of the invaders and their omnipresent spies. The speeches comprise one of the most important texts in the literature of nationalism. In order to raise German morale, the philosopher-turned-polemicist dwelt on the unique spiritual properties of the momentarily defeated Germans, and their special mission – in American terms 'manifest destiny' – to chart the future course of European civilization. Europe was in crisis: a soulless modernity, embodied in the "neo-Latin" French, threatened to stifle the richer, nobler values of its founding peoples, i.e., the old Germanic tribes and their descendants, for Napoleonic imperialism was cultural as well as military.

Among modern Europeans, according to Fichte, only the Germans managed to preserve their originality of being and hence their racial authenticity. Only the Germans were still nourished by the hidden springs of life itself, or life in its true invisible essence. They alone could be deemed an *Urvolk*, a primordial people. They alone possessed an *Ursprache*, a primordial and original language, an uncorrupted mother tongue. Languages are either living or dead, either in communion with nature and the divine origins of life or separated from their organic and spiritual roots (a dead language can still be spoken). French, a neo-Latin language, was dead; its beauty, like that of French culture itself, was only the beauty of cut flowers, fragile and superficial. German, on the other hand, was a living language, for, unlike the French – the Frankish founders of the French kingdom were Germanic – the Germans had not exchanged their Teutonic birthright for Roman pottage, retaining instead the natal European tongue and its rich expressive tones. Therefore Germany was the last authentic culture in Europe, the only bearer of spirit, the particular in which the universal was enshrined, the elect nation. The God-inspired German genius, in the philosopher's extravagant words, possessed the wings of an eagle and could soar into the empyrean, whereas the neo-Latin genius was a mere sylph (hummingbird) by comparison.[15]

With such pictorial and picturesque images, Fichte, the protégé of Immanuel Kant, spoke of Germany, not the actual Germany of assorted kingdoms, duchies and city-states but the larger spiritual Germany that transcended political boundaries, the true German nation. Nations are immaterial as well as material, and the true German nation, the repository of all goodness and virtue, was as real and substantial in his mind as the Poland of the Polish patriots who wove German ideas into Polish nationalism. It was the German vocation to renew European civilization, returning freedom and the 'kingdom of reason' to the nations, but moral progress could only be realized if the Germans first reformed themselves, instilling lofty patriotic ideals into their children through the schools and universities. In his educational proposals, Fichte, no doubt consciously, cast himself in the role of a German Plato, the educator of the Germans as Plato had been the educator of the Greeks. Consequently his speeches can be read in a comparative light to the ancient philosopher's *Republic*, however repugnant much of their content to modern sensibilities. (Of course, Plato's ideas are also repugnant to modern critics who detect a decided whiff of totalitarianism in his prescriptions for the ideal state.[16])

Like Fichte, the nationalist poet Arndt greatly feared French imperialism, especially French cultural imperialism and its linguistic threat to the German language and thus the German soul that loomed with Napoleon's conquests. "If the French possess the Rhine they possess the heart of our people, they attack us in our innermost being, they destroy us in the germ of our life," he declared in one of his political tracts.[17] Germany, the true Germany, to extend the metaphor, was in danger of crucifixion. Therefore the Germans must unite in defence of their spiritual and material nation, their fatherland:

Where is the German fatherland?
Is't Prussia, or the Swabian land?
Where by the Rhine the grapes are growing?
Or where the Baltic waves are flowing
　　Oh no! More grand,

Far wider is our fatherland!
Where is the German fatherland?
Declare to us where is that land:
As far as 'neath the spreading skies
Our German hymns to God arise -
    All that wide land,
Brave brothers, call our fatherland!

All Germany we call our own!
May God behold it from His throne;
And give to all who in it dwell
True hearts to love and cherish well
    All this wide land –
All Germany, our fatherland![18]

This well-known poem *Des Deutschen Vaterland* was written in 1813 during the epic war of liberation when, set to music, it became a battle-song.[19] God, Arndt believed, was on the side of German arms, for God, it seems, had German affinities; indeed, God was almost if not quite a Germanic deity. It was therefore in the nature of things for the "German God" to promote the freedom of the German nation.[20] By nation, of course, Arndt meant the cultural and linguistic Germany of the spirit that presaged the Germany of the flesh, or the political confederation that even the early nationalists hoped would arise to replace the multiple German states. This included the strange dream of a new German emperor – Friedrich Barbarossa *redivivus* – a popular feature of nine-teenth-century German romanticism. In his later years, "old 'Father'Arndt, with his aureole of white hair,"[21] for whom Germany had thirty princes too many, continued to worry about French aggression at the hands of Napoleon III: "Oh, our Germany! Do we have to look into a dark future?"[22] The shadow of a national cross still fell across the banks of the Rhine; the French were still seen as potential crucifiers.

In the case of Schleiermacher (incidentally, Arndt's brother-in-law), no small measure of the great theologian's fervent nationalism was gener-ated by his personal anger at the military occupation of Halle in 1806, when French soldiers were quartered in his own lodgings. The threat to shut down the University of Halle where he taught cast his career into limbo, and he faced what has been described as one of his darkest hours.[23] Physical deprivation – the war had ravaged the German economy – as well as national humiliation intensified his sense of alienation and thus (like Fichte) his antagonism toward the rival nation despite his youthful idealistic admiration (also like Fichte) for the French Revolution. Such was his bitterness that, in contrast to his famous contemporary Hegel, who gazed with admiration when Napoleon rode in triumph through the streets of Jena ("I saw the Emperor – this world-soul . . . It is indeed a wonderful sensation to see such an individual, who . . . astride a horse, reaches out over the world and masters it"[24]), Schleiermacher refused to watch the victor's triumphal procession in Halle. Prussia had been defeated, but Prussia was not a nation, only a state; Germany, the larger cultural, linguistic and spiritual community, was a nation, despite its many political divisions, and God, Schleiermacher believed, loves nations as much as individuals, and especially loves the German nation. A new Germany was destined to arise out of the ashes of the old Germany, a better and more beautiful Germany conceived, nurtured and guided by divine providence. "Bless those who will live to see it; but those who die, may they die in faith."[25] As in ancient times, the suffering of God's chosen people held a hidden meaning both as chastisement and as a test of faith. God had not abandoned Germany any more than God had abandoned biblical Israel, or, for that matter, Jesus on his cross. However, the Germans, including Schleiermacher himself, were required to devote themselves to patriotic causes, which meant working for national unification. As a step in the right direction, the theologian, a small and slightly malformed man unfit for much physical exertion, even involved himself in clandestine activities in Berlin, joining an anti-French secret society in order to assist in the expulsion of the invaders.*

Along with his incisive intellect, Schleiermacher was an orator *extraordinaire*, and his sermons, which reveal his nationalist beliefs, played no small part in the stirring of patriotic emotions in Prussia. On one occasion in 1813, according to an eye-witness account, his "sonorous, clear and penetrating voice" reduced a regiment of Prussian soldiers in Berlin on the eve of battle to tears while extolling the glories of sacrificing one's life for the fatherland.[26] Like Fichte, only from the vantage point of the Protestant pulpit, he sought to inculcate nationalistic and patriotic values; like Fichte, he saw himself as a public educator:

> As we ourselves have been most deeply moved by the distress and humiliation of the past years, and the glorious resurrection of the Fatherland in these days, let us also impress all this most strongly on the rising generation; that this eternally memorable time may indeed be remembered, and that each descendant whom it concerns may say with just pride, there fought, or there fell, a relation of mine.[27]

★ The Charlottenburger Verein.

Dulce et decorum est pro patria mori! ★

The Germans, Schleiermacher had little doubt, like the biblical Israelites, had been singled out for a special destiny: they were God's chosen.[28] As a result, their war of liberation was really a species of holy war, a term that the preacher-theologian did not shrink from employing.[29] God may indeed chastise Germany as God had once chastised Israel, but the chosen nation will never be destroyed. So intimate is the bond between the national community and the Christian faith that a lack of proper devotion to one's country condemns the disloyal subject to alien status in the house of God.[30] That such a dogma could have been enunciated by a reformed (non-Lutheran) theologian reveals much about the age. True patriotism and true Christianity are joined together, but the former is dominant: a fusion that in its extreme form produced the political idolatry of Nazi times. Had he anticipated its final poisonous fruit, the humane eighteenth-century theologian would have been horrified. In a another sermon, preached in Berlin in 1818 on the anniversary of the Battle of Leipzig (the Battle of the Nations) – a battle that assumed mythical proportions in German nationalistic historiography because of the German victory over Napoleon – Schleiermacher heaped scorn on those unpatriotic Prussians who had not thrown their weight wholeheartedly behind the military effort against the French.[31] They were bad Germans and, by implication, bad Christians as well and did not deserve to participate in the national jubilation.

The powerful religious and quasi-religious belief in German election, cultivated and nurtured during times of adversity, was deepened with the final defeat and overthrow of Napoleon, whose fall at Waterloo some Protestant preachers likened to the fall of Nebuchadnezzar:[32] "How you are fallen from heaven, O Day Star, Son of Dawn! How you are cut down to the ground, you who laid the nations low!"† God, the biblical God, had spoken, and God's chosen, God's *Favoritvolk*, the German Israelites, had seen the skies open and the divine hand intervene in the affairs of the world, piercing the mortal veil. Germany now started to become holy Germany, and the cause of German unification started to become a sacred duty as well as a desirable constitutional goal. When another Napoleon threatened a still divided Germany in 1870, and when the new Nebuchadnezzar suffered the same fate as his predecessor, falling to the ground (at least figuratively) before the armies of the Lord, the faith of the pious nationalists was doubly vindicated. The Kingdom of Prussia became the Protestant "Holy of Holies" and the elevation of the Prussian

★ It is sweet and seemly to die for one's country.
† Isaiah 14:12.

king to the throne of the second German empire as Wilhelm I in 1871 became the linchpin of a heavenly design.[33] Otto von Bismarck, the iron chancellor who forged the reconstituted Reich, was an unlikely servant of spiritual and supernatural ends, but even his critics saw the hand of providence in his actions, invoking the divine spirit behind current events and the "divine judgment of Sedan."[34] The lessons of history are conclusive. Had not the Germans been selected over the French? Had they not been found worthy to establish a new Christian Reich in "the tradition of the Carolingian Empire?"[35] So many pious believed. The Germans and the Germans alone were the true children of God. The influential Berlin historian, Heinrich von Treitschke, who in his youth had sat at the feet of Arndt, regarded rival England as a "new Carthage," as much an obstacle in the path of Germany's march to greatness as ancient Carthage had been an obstacle to Roman ambitions.[36] His entranced students at the University of Berlin evidently regarded their professor himself as a Siegfried-figure![37]

This image of Germany as a latter-day Israel became almost an article of faith in the German churches, especially those of a pietistic bent, from whence it spread into the political arena.[38] In the eyes of nationalistic churchmen, a new covenant had been inaugurated between God and the German nation, a covenant based on the biblical model of the covenant with Israel, but easily transformed into a less biblical manifesto of Germanic superiority.[39] Not all Germans, of course, were devout, at least in the Christian sense, and some were driven by other dreams and visions, notably the racial mythologies that were gaining popularity in the late nineteenth century, but they also endorsed the national vision. Richard Wagner (1813–1883), the great operatic composer, was, by his own admission,[40] influenced by Count Arthur de Gobineau's treatise on human inequality (*Essai sur l'inégalité des races humaines*) and used the latter's racial theories to reinforce his romantic glorification of the Germanic *Volk*. Steeped also in the Grimm brothers and old Teutonic myths and legends, Wagner saw the gods and heroes of the sagas as personifications of the German race-spirit and interwove pagan and Christian themes in some of his operas, especially the Ring cycle.

> In the German Volk survives the oldest lawful race of Kings in all the world: it issues from a son of God, called by his nearest kinsmen Siegfried, but Christ by the remaining nations of the earth; for the welfare of his race, and the peoples of the earth derived therefrom, he wrought a deed most glorious, and for that deed's sake suffered death.[41]

It follows that Siegfried, the archetypal German who, significantly, is murdered, is intended as a Christ-figure, and Germany, by implication, is intended as the Christ-nation, that is to say, the nation descended from Siegfried, the "stem-god" or ancestral deity of the German (Aryan) race. Not without reason did the composer regard himself as an evangelist of German redemption and his music as its instrument. Not without reason did both his religiosity and his nationalism draw the scorn of the anti-Christian, anti-nationalist Friedrich Nietzsche who, for all his own serious failings, saw the stupidity in the "Christian-romantic" obsessions of German society, of which Wagner, his onetime friend, had made himself a high priest with his reanimation of the old "Scandinavian monsters" of song and saga.[42] Both the pseudo-Christian opera *Parsifal* and the four operas of the *Ring* cycle with their gods, giants, dwarves, water-maidens and Valkyries represent a strange brew of Christian and Teutonic ingredients in which the latter reign supreme. At least initially, as George Bernard Shaw recognized, the entire cycle was intended as a social and political allegory of the modern world, a quasi-political "drama of today."[43] As far as Nietzsche was concerned, neither Christianity nor Teutonism nor any combination or synthesis of the two augured well for the health and moral well-being of the German psyche.

Christian romanticism, however, assisted by Wagner's 'holy German art,' was assuredly on the rise. It permeated much political thought, combined with a powerful strain of what can only be described as Germanic self-pity as, for example, when Treitschke routinely burst into tears during his lectures while recounting the sufferings of his country at foreign hands.[44] The Thirty Years' War was his favourite subject for lachrymose displays. Self-pity is a regular feature of romantic pathos, and one easily associated with crucifixion themes. It is the other side of self-exaltation, and Treitschke was not alone in his national anguish; many others, especially many churchmen, thought in similar terms, both in the nineteenth and twentieth centuries. Not self-pity but "boundless self-pity" – the expression belongs to Fritz Stern[45] – found many opportunities for public expression in modern times. The First World War (1914–18), otherwise known as the Great War, which German patriots saw as a continuation of the war of liberation against Napoleon, supplied one such occasion.[46] Although the new war of liberation began on a note of celebration, as wars so often do, it ended on a far darker note, as wars also so often do. The initial joyous mood was vibrant, a veritable "nationalist orgy" involving all classes of German society, the educated and the uneducated alike.[47] Rapturous speeches and sermons greeted the German war declarations (against Russia on August 1, France on August 3, Belgium on August 4); not only were most Germans united in their war fever, they were united also in the certainty that their cause was righteous and that sacrificial death for the sake of the fatherland was Christian and noble. While there were notable exceptions, the sentiment was widespread. Ninety-three German intellectuals, including a number of famous theologians, endorsed the war policies of the emperor and his ministers in a public manifesto, and one of the signatories, the eminent church historian Adolf von Harnack, composed the war speech delivered by Wilhelm II from the balcony of his palace in Berlin. Thus did the Protestant establishment choose to sanctify the national call to arms. To those who had read Hegel, not to mention Fichte and Schleiermacher, and had listened to Wagner's music, August 1914 seemed a world-historical moment, a moment that confirmed Germany's election, a moment in which the Almighty was unmistakably present, a moment reminiscent of other God-filled moments in the sacred history of the German nation: 1517, 1813, 1870.[48] Some war enthusiasts knew no bounds in their utterances:

We may become frightened, but the history of our nation steps before us and consoles us: 'You will not die, but live; you will not perish, but be preserved.' Only have courage, land of the Teutons! Only have courage, sons and daughters of Germany! Endure! Stand fast! The God of old still lives, the God who has so many times brought storms to our country. He is with you. He will not forsake you. Only do not forsake him. You will not die, but live.[49]

With such sentiments all too common, it is little wonder that the 'passion' of Germany in 1914–1918 was compared to the passion of Christ, for Germany, like Christ, was faced with assassination by the unrighteous powers of the world, meaning, of course, England, France and Russia.[50] As God was disclosed in the original crucifixion, God was also disclosed in its modern re-enactment. In keeping with this far from modest view of things, the emperor himself was compared by one zealous pastor to Christ, for, alone among the rulers of the great powers, Wilhelm II was truly devout, bowing the knee to God rather than man; unlike the idolatrous British, for example, the emperor, like Christ, could say: "They hated me without a cause."[51] When the German armies started to win battles (prior to the Battle of the Marne), the conviction of a hidden hand at work grew stronger, deepening the faith of the devout. God's covenant with Germany was placed in sharp historical relief. The Holy

Spirit, the same Holy Spirit associated with Pentecost, was revealed once again, for the war was nothing less than a Pentecost experience for the German nation, "a time full of pentecostal power for a pentecostal work."[52] Indeed, according to one participant in the ecstatic rallies of the time, August 4, 1914 (the day of national mobilization) witnessed a sudden rushing from heaven, sweeping away all divisions and leaving the Germans united as they had never been united before: "I see no more parties," declared the emperor, "I see only Germans!"[53] These became Wilhelm II's most famous words.

The emperor's beatific vision was short-lived. During the next four years, Germany suffered 2,000,000 casualties, with another 4,000,000 wounded, many maimed for life, causing the euphoria of the early days to vanish into thin air. Having expected the best, the nation was forced to face the worst, a turn of events not calculated to improve the national morale. When in 1918 the prospect of total defeat and alien armies on German soil became evident to realists in both the army and the state, a new German government under Prince Max von Baden reluctantly sued for peace. A cascade of tumultuous events soon engulfed the nation: navy mutiny, political disintegration, the abdication and flight of the emperor, the proclamation of a republic, impending revolution (the Spartacists), military repression, and, in 1919, what John Maynard Keynes called the "Carthaginian" peace imposed by the victors at Versailles. Not only were the terms of the treaty regarded as vindictive by the vanquished Germans – especially the bitterly resented war guilt clause – but so also was the site chosen by the victors for the signing ceremony on June 28: the Hall of Mirrors in the great palace of the French kings that Bismarck had selected for the inauguration rites of the reconstituted German empire in 1871. Bismarck's choice was not accidental; Louis XIV, the builder of Versailles, as every German schoolboy knew, had invaded German lands and devastated the Palatinate over a century before Napoleon, humiliating the German princes.★ In retaliation for Louis XIV (and Napoleon), the Prussians had sought to humiliate the French. In retaliation for Sedan, the French, led by Georges Clemenceau, with the acquiescence of David Lloyd George, fully intended to humiliate the Germans.

Humiliation, real or imagined, is always a powerful fuel of nationalism. It stirs a dangerous desire to reverse the verdicts of history at any cost. It creates and nurtures a politics of resentment (*ressentiment*) both within nations and between nations. Western resentment of Germany

★ The War of the League of Augsburg.

and German resentment of the Keynesian Carthaginian peace did much to undermine the Weimar Republic erected on the ruins of the Second Reich, with consequences that do not require much elaboration. When General Paul von Hindenberg told a post-war inquiry in 1919 that the German army had been stabbed in the back, he provided his country, especially its angry elites, with a lethal new legend, one that Adolf Hitler was later to exploit to his personal advantage. To the Christian romantic nationalists, the stab-in-the-back theory evoked an obvious New Testament analogue, although, in fact, Hindenburg himself preferred to blame socialist anti-war machinations on the home front for the "secret mutilation" of the German armed forces; he allowed others to blame the Jews.[54] The stab-in-the-back theory also evoked the Wagnerian hero Siegfried, the archetypal idealized German, the "unsuspecting, naive hero cut down by the scheming villainous Hagen,"[55] a capitalist-socialist-Judas-Jew such as the antisemites of the day loved to hate. Having already compared the German plight to Jesus in Gethsemane in patriotic war sermons and speeches, it was not difficult for the Protestant leadership, as well as many other Germans, to assign the outcome of the military struggle to Judas-like acts of treachery.[56] As the churches were generally cast in a conservative and authoritarian mould (both theologically and politically), this conclusion was fairly congenial; subservience to the state was a legacy of the Lutheran reformation springing from the reformer's high regard for temporal authority. If one did not wish to believe that the German armies had been stalemated on the battlefield, solace could be found in the notion of betrayal. The Judas–Hagen motif probably also played a part in the assassination of Walther Rathenau (1922), the Jewish foreign minister, and acquired even more sinister overtones during the Great Depression and its economic woes.

In their synthesis of Christianity and the "inner (German) fatherland,"[57] however, some patriotic German Christians were prepared to acknowledge that holy Germany had contributed to its own downfall, betrayal or no betrayal. The elect people, the same people who in August, 1914, consumed as they thought by pentecostal fire,[58] had welcomed the war, nevertheless played an unwitting part in its sorry end. They accused themselves of failing to sustain the noble spirit of sacrifice of its heady beginning, the chorus of effusion and national solidarity that had moved the emperor. This failure was a sin, and God surely punishes sins. In permitting Germany's defeat, God, the Lord of history, had punished his *Favoritvolk*, rebuking the Germans as of old the same God had once rebuked biblical Israel for its sins. The conclusion was painful but not without its appeal since it reinforced the proud hubristic assumptions of the pious nationalists.

It appealed, for example, to a number of prominent theologians, including the highly esteemed Emanuel Hirsch of the University of Göttingen.[59] Protestant teaching no less than Protestant preaching was still strongly coloured with nationalistic tints, one symptom of which was the far-from-subtle transformation of Martin Luther himself into a Teutonic hero by ultra-patriotic modern Lutherans.[60] Luther himself had lived before the age of nationalism and was neither a nationalist nor even a proto-nationalist as the term is properly understood. This fact, however, did not deter his latter-day admirers. Along with many other Germans, these theological professors had little love for the Weimar Republic which they typically saw as corrupt, decadent and godless, a nest of atheists and traitors. Hirsch, who had also preached patriotic sermons during the war years, investing German arms with divine sanctity, and who had hoped and prayed for a German victory up to the last minute, found defeat a bitter cup to swallow, indeed a genuine test of faith itself.[61] Yet, despite his personal anguish, he never doubted the fidelity of the transcendent deity and the hidden meaning of the sorrows inflicted on the elect. Holy Germany had been disobedient – even the 1918 revolution against the Christian emperor was seen as an act of disobedience[62] – but God was gracious and merciful, and the day of national vindication and resurrection was certain to come.

That day came or seemed to come on January 30, 1933 when another pentecostal moment, another divine visitation or, in Hirsch's memorable words, a "great holy storm" (*grosser heiliger Sturm*) swept Germany in the form of the National Socialist revolution, bringing to the chancellorship a new Moses designated by God to lead the elect Germans out of their historical wilderness.[63] His name was Adolf Hitler. The Protestant theologian, who drew many of his core ideas from Fichte, on whose thought he was an expert, was utterly transfixed:

> The 'yes' to this hour is alive within me as a heart-felt gratitude to God, who after a long period of shame and darkness has appeared to us like a fire. If tomorrow the Führer calls us to show allegiance to the new National Socialist Germany, man to man, woman to woman, we will answer yes. I will say yes as a German, as an Evangelical Christian and theologian, as a university professor. I will say it as one small voice in the great chorus which responds to the call of the Führer: We will say yes, we will follow him. Heil Hitler![64]

The Führer himself, a consummate actor, knew how to play the role of a 'Christian' leader perfectly when it suited his purposes, even closing a speech on one occasion with a prayer (May 1, 1933). Hirsch and other patriotic churchmen were much impressed by Hitler's piety.[65]

Alas, the devout theologian, a good and moral man but a dupe easily deceived by a charlatan, was, along with many of his generation, profoundly mistaken; another period of shame and darkness, more terrible than the former, was soon to descend. By the time that Hitler's '1000 year' Reich collapsed in 1945, 4,500,000 Germans lay dead, and the great cities of Germany, including Berlin, lay in ruins, a devastation more terrible than even that suffered during the Thirty Years' War, the previous worst chapter in German history. Not without reason, the period between 1914 and 1945 is sometimes described as a second Thirty Years' War.[66] Many Germans, like Treitschke in the nineteenth century, found ample reason to shed tears for their fatherland and its fate. One Treitschke-like elegist was Otto Dibelius, Protestant bishop of Berlin, an old fashioned patriot for whom the defeat of 1918 had been bad enough – he had originally welcomed the Great War as God's 'great wedding feast'![67] – but not as bad as the unconditional surrender in 1945. The inhumanity and "moral distress" of a divided fatherland (east and west) was a cross almost too heavy for his wounded soul to bear.[68] Had the victorious allies once again been cruel and vindictive? Had they once again humiliated the defeated Germans, particularly by placing 16,000,000 of the latter under an atheistic and alien tyranny – an "anti-Christian archpontificate" in the bishop's words[69] – determined to stamp out the churches and the Word of God? Beyond question they had, as far as Dibelius was concerned, although diplomatic considerations prevented him from speaking in this direct fashion to foreign Christians.[70] However, as a nationalist nurtured in the old school of holy Germany, he could not relinquish the proud assumptions of the past. Overwhelmed by German suffering, which was genuine enough – one recalls the bombing of Dresden, February 13, 1945 – Dibelius found it difficult if not impossible to speak of the suffering inflicted by Germans on others, and had to be reminded of the latter.[71] His silence on this uncomfortable topic was typical of many of his contemporaries.

The suffering inflicted by Germans on others, as anyone with a conscience knew – the bishop did in fact possess a conscience – had to be acknowledged, even if reluctantly, for the truth could not be suppressed; the evidence of the death camps was incontestable, although a soon-to-arise new generation of antisemites nonetheless conspired to contest it. Jews and Gypsies were the most palpable victims of crucifixion and the most horribly tortured. Because of these crimes, the worldview that had informed the old certitudes and had generated the stab-in-the-back theory of 1919 was largely shattered; no such theory was employed in 1945 by angry generals in order to excuse their military failures. Instead, a different note was struck, at least in some religious circles, resulting in the Stuttgart Confession of Guilt (*Stuttgarter Schuldbekenntnis*) of the German Protestant Church Council: "With great pain do we say: through us (Germans) endless suffering has been brought to many peoples and countries."[72] These simple words swept away the treasured quasi-religious, quasi-political belief in German special status, nourished and cultivated in German Protestantism since Fichte and Schleiermacher.[73] There were numerous voices of dissent, of course, as less repentant Germans railed against the Protestant confession, accusing its authors of preparing the ground for another Versailles.[74] German virtue and German innocence (of the nation if not of the regime) were still eternal truths in many minds. On the other hand, many others were truly contrite, especially in the churches which now started to become pockets of resistance to the East German communist police state, perhaps, as has been suggested, in atonement for past failures.[75] Their contrition served to dissipate self-pity and therefore hubristic self-inflation, the self-righteous pride of those accustomed to placing themselves on a pedestal. For this reason, the Stuttgart Confession of 1945 cannot be dismissed as a minor and inconsequential moment in German history. It was a moment of glory.

Radical changes occurred in subsequent time. German prosperity was restored in the Bonn Republic under Konrad Adenauer and his financial wizard Ludwig Erhard, the ruined cities were rebuilt, the European Common Market (now the European Union) came into existence, the hated Berlin Wall fell in 1989 and, prompted by Soviet decline and economic troubles in its satellite state, the two estranged Germanys were reunited in 1990, even if festering resentments and serious social troubles continued to plague the restored single nation. Some critics, especially in the east, regarded and still regard the unification as imposed by the west and thus in effect another *Anschluss* reminiscent of the Nazi seizure of Austria in 1938.[76] Despite this shadow, it signified for most Germans the dawn of a hopeful new era. Old myths, however, die hard, and deeply ingrained sentiments are not easily eradicated. While the proud nationalism of the past has been repudiated, at least in official discourse, nationalistic dreams and fantasies have not vanished entirely from German society. Discordant notes continue to sound, especially as the post-Nazi generation struggles with the spectre of the Third Reich and its crimes: an albatross simply too heavy for some German necks. Those unable to accept the painful facts exposed by the Nürnberg trials have found, like the philosopher-historian Ernst Nolte,[77] ingenious ways of diminishing their significance. Less sophisticated old-style nationalists have turned to radical new parties with strident manifestos, notably the *National Demokratische Partei Deutschlands* and the *Republikaner Partei*. Romantic Fichtean language about the Germanic *Volk* has been invoked by these factions to rekindle atavistic feelings with slogans such as "Germany for the Germans – Europe for the Europeans."[78] 'Europe for the Europeans' represents a reaction against the rising tide of alien immigrants in Europe in recent decades, drawing together ultra right politicians in various nations. Thus Franz Schönhuber, the leader of the *Republikaner Partei*, had no difficulty on one occasion in walking arm in arm with Jean-Marie Le Pen, old Franco-German animosities notwithstanding; their antipathies have merged.[79] While holy Germany, Christian-romantic Germany, imperial Germany with its sacral union between altar and throne, the idealized Germany of Schleiermacher, Arndt and Fichte, the Germany of Bismarck and Treitschke, is no more, its *volkisch* ghost still lingers. As long as its presence is felt, joined by the ghost of Adolf Hitler, unrepentant children will be bred.

Notes

1 Cited in Karl Hammer, *Deutsche Kriegs-Theologie 1870–1918*, München: Kösel-Verlag, 1971, p. 214. My translation.

2 Cited in Franz Kohler, *Die deutsche protestantische Kriegspredigt der Gegenwart dargestellt in ihrer homiletischen Eigenart*, Giessen, 1915, pp. 54, 55. German Catholics were also nationalistic, but ambivalent toward the Protestant monarchy and resentful of Bismarck's Kulturkampf.

3 Ibid., p. 55.

4 Dietrich Vorwerk, *Was sagt der Weltkrieg den deutschen Christen?*, Schwerin, Mecklenburg, 1915, p. 34.

5 Ibid., p. 34. My translation.

6 Cf. Hartmut Lehmann, "'God Our Old Ally': The Chosen People Theme in Late Nineteenth- and Early Twentieth-Century German Nationalism," *Many Are Chosen: Divine Election and Western Nationalism*, William R. Hutchison & Hartmut Lehmann (eds), Minneapolis: Fortress Press, 1994, pp. 105–106.

7 Cf. Fritz Stern, *Five Germanys I have Known*, New York: Farrar, Strauss & Giroux, 2006, p. 103.

8 W. R. Ward, ibid., p. 53.

9 Sir Isaiah Berlin, "Nationalism; past neglect and present power," *Against the*

Current: Essays in the History of Ideas, Oxford: Oxford University Press, 1981, p. 350.

10 See, for example, Hans Kohn, *The Idea of Nationalism: A Study in its Origins and Background*, Toronto: Collier Books, 1967, pp. 334–348.

11 Norman Cohn, *The Pursuit of the Millennium*, New York: Oxford University Press, 1970, p. 119f.

12 Ibid., p. 457.

13 Sir Isaiah Berlin, *Three Critics of the Enlightenment: Vico, Hamann, Herder*, Princeton: Princeton University Press, 2000, p. 208.

14 Johann Gottfried von Herder, *Philosophical Writings*, trans. Michael N. Forster, Cambridge: Cambridge University Press, p. 385.

15 Johann Gottlieb Fichte, *Reden an die deutsche Nation*, trans. R. F. Jones & G. H. Turnbull. ed. George Armstrong Kelly, New York: Harper & Row, 1968, pp. 73–74 Fichte declares: "So we may say that genius in foreign lands will strew with flowers the well-trodden military roads of antiquity, and weave a becoming robe for that wisdom of life which it will easily take for philosophy. The German spirit, on the other hand, will open up new shafts and bring the light of day into their abysses, and hurl up rocky masses of thoughts, out of which ages to come will build their dwellings."

16 Plato has many detractors, most famously Sir Karl Popper, *The Open Society and its Enemies*, Vol. I, 1962.

17 Cited in Alfred G. Pundt, *Arndt and the Nationalist Awakening in Germany*, New York: AMS Press, 1968, p. 118.

18 Ibid. (cited), p. 98.

19 It was Ludwig Jahn, the promoter of gymnastics and author of *Das deutsche Volkstum*, who turned Arndt's poem into a battle-song.

20 Ibid., p. 166.

21 James Elstone Dow, *A Good German Conscience: The Life and Times of Ernst Moritz Arndt*, Lanham: University Press of America, 1995, p. 129.

22 Ibid. (cited), p. 128.

23 Cf. Jerry F. Dawson, *Friedrich Schleiermacher: The Evolution of a Nationalist*, Austin: University of Texas Press, 1966, p. 62.

24 Letter to Niethammer, October 13, 1806.

25 Letter to Karl August Varnhagen, November 17, 1806. Cited in Martin Redeker, *Schleiermacher: Life and Thought*, trans. John Wallhauser, Philadelphia: Fortress Press, 1973, p. 86.

26 See Koppel S. Pinson, *Pietism as a Factor in the Rise of German Nationalism*, New York: Columbia University Press, 1934, p. 11.

27 "A Nation's Duty in a War for Freedom," *Selected Sermons of Schleiermacher*, trans. Mary F. Wilson, New York: Funk & Wagnalls, n.d., p. 79.

28 Dawson, op. cit., p. 83.

29 "A Nation's Duty in a War for Freedom," *Selected Sermons*, p. 69.

30 Pinson, op. cit., p. 98.

31 See Dawson, op. cit., pp. 140–141.

32 Arlie J. Hoover, *The Gospel of Nationalism: German Patriotic Preaching from*

    Napoleon to Versailles, Stuttgart: Franz Steiner Verlag Wiesbaden GMBH, 1986, p. 36

33 Ibid., p. 43.

34 Cf. Andreas Dorpalen, *Heinrich von Treitschke*, New Haven: Yale University Press, 1957, p.173.

35 Uriel Tal, *Christians and Jews in Germany: Religion, Politics and Ideology in the Second Reich, 1870–1914*, trans. Noah Jonathan Jacobs, Ithaca: Cornell University Press, 1975, p. 257.

36 Louis L. Snyder, *German Nationalism: The Tragedy of a People*, Harrisburg: Stackpole, 1952, p. 147.

37 Ibid., p. 143.

38 Cf. Hartmut Lehmann, op. cit., p. 102.

39 Ibid., p. 104.

40 See Wagner's essay "Herodom and Christendom," *Richard Wagner's Prose Works*, trans. William Ashton Ellis, New York: Broude Brothers, 1966 (reprinted from 1898 edition), Vol. VI, p. 275f.

41 See Wagner, "The Nibelungen," op. cit., Vol. VII, p. 289.

42 Friedrich Nietzsche, *Beyond Good and Evil*, Part VIII, 251. See also Nietzsche's late tirade against his ex friend *Nietzsche contra Wagner* (1895).

43 George Bernard Shaw, *The Perfect Wagnerite: A Commentary on the Niblung's Ring*, New York: Dover, 1967, p. i. As a composer of genius, Wagner was a complex figure and the Ring operas are far too rich in suggestion and meaning to be confined to a single mode of interpretation. Besides political and social allegory, they also provide rich fare for psychological analysis or the journey of self-discovery, especially the themes of love and incest, and are usually read and staged in this light. Wagner's personal interest seems to have shifted from political to metaphysical themes as he wrote and rewrote the four operas of the cycle, enlarging and deepening the meaning of the symbols and myths incorporated into the narrative. Myth and psychology, of course, are closely intertwined, and Wagner adopted the romantic view that the tales of the gods were really parables of the human soul. Here also the crucifixion motif comes into play, as when the god Wotan hangs himself on the Tree of Life and descends into the dark underworld as Christ descended into hell. The composer was variously influenced by Bakunin, Schopenhauer and Feuerbach and their assorted ideas about the nature of life, religion and the world. For a mostly psychoanalytic (Jungian) exposition, see Robert Donnington, *Wagner's 'Ring' and its Symbols: The Music and the Myth*, London: Faber & Faber, 1963. For a good introduction, see M. Owen Lee, *Wagner's Ring*, New York: Limelight Editions, 1990. Wagner, however, was never really consistent, even in his political ideas; no true system can be abstracted from his work, although the general contours of his mind, especially his early revolutionary instincts and his fervent nationalism ('holy German art'), are clear enough. So, unfortunately, is his vicious antisemitism. For another excellent study, see Ronald Taylor, *Richard Wagner: His Life, Art and Thought*, London: Paul Elek, 1979.

44   Dorpalen, op. cit., p. 239.

45   Fritz Stern, *The Failure of Illiberalism: Essays on the Political Culture of Modern Germany*, New York: Alfred A. Knopf, 1972, p. 219.

46   Cf. A. J. Hoover, *God, Germany and Britain in the Great War: A Study in Clerical Nationalism*, New York: Praeger, 1989, p. 53.

47   Fritz Stern, *Five Germanys I have Known*, p. 37.

48   See the excellent essay by A. J. Hoover, "German Christian Nationalism: Its Contribution to the Holocaust," *Remembering for the Future* (Theme I), International Scholars' Conference, Oxford, July 10–13, 1988, pp. 62–71.

49   A. J. Hoover, *The Gospel of Nationalism* (cited), p. 52.

50   Ibid., p. 48.

51   Hoover, *God, Britain and Germany in the Great War*, p. 78. The reference is to John 15:25.

52   Hoover, *The Gospel of Nationalism* (cited), p. 77.

53   Ibid.

54   As cited in *The Weimar Republic Sourcebook*, Anton Kaes, Martin Jay, Edward Dimendberg (eds), Berkeley: University of California Press, 1994, pp. 15–16.

55   Stern, op. cit., p. 11, fn. 4.

56   Cf. Kenneth C. Barnes, *Nazism, Liberalism and Christianity: Protestant Social Thought in Germany and Great Britain 1925–1937*, Lexington: University Press of Kentucky, 1991, p. 36.

57   Cf. George L. Mosse, *The Nationalization of the Masses: Political Symbolism and Mass Movements in Germany from the Napoleonic Wars through the Third Reich*, New York: Howard Fertig, 1975, p. 74.

58   It has to be noted that even liberal scholars and theologians as eminent as Ernst Troeltsch and Adolf von Harnack were highly nationalistic and believed in the Germanic *Volk* and the pentecostal fires of 1914. See Hoover, *The Gospel of Nationalism*, p. 51.

59   Cf. Gunda Schneider-Flume, *Die politische Theologie Emanuel Hirschs, 1918–1933*, Bern: Herbert Lang, 1971, pp. 2–3.

60   C. James M. Stayer, *Martin Luther, German Saviour: German Evangelical Theological Factions and the Interpretation of Luther, 1917–1933*, Kingston & Montreal: McGill–Queen's University Press.

61   Robert P. Ericksen, *Theologians Under Hitler: Gerhard Kittel, Paul Althaus and Emanuel Hirsch*, New Haven: Yale University Press, 1985, p. 125.

62   Cf. A. James Reimer, *The Emanuel Hirsch and Paul Tillich Debate: A Study in the Political Ramifications of Theology*, Lewiston: Edwin Mellen Press, 1989, p. 54.

63   Schneider-Flume, op. cit., p. 160.

64   Cited in Reimer, op. cit., p. 57, fn. 17. My translation (I have altered Reimer's translation which appears on the same page). As this citation reveals, Hirsch was an extraordinary case of self-delusion on the part of a man of great brilliance, great learning and high personal morals. Despite these qualities, he was devoted to an evil political order which he simply

did not recognize as evil, believing to the end of his days that God had sent Hitler. This myopia can only be described as a tragedy of monumental proportions and a testimony to the demonic power of nationalism in the modern world. Despite the possession of an exceptional mind, he can be regarded as an illustration of Hannah Arendt's provocative thesis that the true root of evil lies in an inability or refusal to think (Arendt, *The Life of the Mind*). At the very least, he confirms what has long been recognized in the history of ideas: intellectual genius is synonymous neither with philosophical sense nor common sense. Paul Tillich and Karl Barth strongly criticized Hirsch for his theological and political misjudgments. Besides the longer studies by Schneider-Flume, Ericksen and Reimer, a good analysis of Hirsch can be found in Jack Forstman, *Christian Faith in Dark Times: Theological Conflicts in the Shadow of Hitler,* Louisville: Westminster/John Knox Press, 1992.

65 Ericksen, op. cit., p. 145.

66 Klaus Scholder, *A Requiem for Hitler*, trans. John Bowden, London: SCM Press, 1989, p. 20.

67 Hoover, *The Gospel of Nationalism*, p. 48.

68 See *In the Service of the Lord: The Autobiography of Bishop Otto Dibelius,* translator Mary Ilford, New York: Holt, Rinehart & Winston, 1964, pp. 236–237.

69 Cf. *Day is Dawning: The Story of Bishop Otto Dibelius Based on His Proclamations and Authentic Documents*, Philadelphia: Christian Education Press, 1956, p. 100.

70 *In the Service of the Lord*, p. 236.

71 Stern, *The Failure of Illiberalism*, p. 220.

72 Cited in Stewart W. Herman, *The Rebirth of the German Church*, New York: Harper & Brothers., 1946, p. 140.

73 Lehmann, op. cit., p. 107.

74 Herman, op. cit., p. 142.

75 Eg., Stern, *Five Germanies I have Known*, p. 421. This subject remains controversial. The churches have also been accused of collaboration with the communist state and the Stasi, acting as police informers against political dissidents. Some East German Protestants with socialist sympathies urged obedience to the state on biblical grounds (Romans 13). Since many of the former had belonged to the anti-Nazi Confessing Church during the Third Reich, they were strongly anti-fascist and highly critical of capitalist and, in their eyes, crypto-fascist West Germany. Because East Germany was by definition anti-fascist, it was seen by such Christians in a different light. For a discussion of this topic, see Gregory Baum, *The Church for Others: Protestant Theology in Communist East Germany*, Grand Rapids: William B. Eerdmans Publishing Co., 1996.

76 Ibid., p. 320.

77 Nolte is a strange and puzzling case. His 1963 book *Three Faces of Fascism* is a brilliant and insightful analysis of the fascist phenomenon in the twentieth

century but his later writings reveal a more nationalistic and apologetic stance, suggesting a quite different turn of mind.

78 See Ivor Montagu, *Germany's New Nazis*, London: Panther Books, 1967, p.127f.

79 Cf, Franz Schönhuber, *Welche Chancen hat die Rechte?*, Coburg: Nation Europa Verlag, 2002, p. 97.

IV

The Crucified Nation
IRELAND

In his impassioned 1916 paean to the spirit of nationalism, *The Sovereign People*, the Irish super-patriot Patrick (Padraig) Pearse (1879–1916) wrote these words:

> Let no man be mistaken as to who will be lord in Ireland when Ireland is free. The people will be lord and master. The people who wept in Gethsemane, who trod the sorrowful way, who died naked on a cross, who went down into hell, will rise again glorious and immortal, will sit on the right hand of God, and will come in the end to give judgment, a judge just and terrible.[1]

The people, the sovereign people, Pearse informs his readers, comprise the nation, a "natural division" as natural as the family and as holy in Catholic eyes, for both the nation and the family are the work of God. This seems simple enough, but a principle of exclusion is embedded in his argument. Like all romantic nationalists Pearse, in the spirit of Emmanuel Joseph Sieyès, casts out of the nation every estate other than the third estate, although he does not employ the French term.[2] Not everyone who dwells on Ireland's sacred shores belongs to the Irish nation, not those "corrupted by England" – the recreant enemies of Irish freedom (usually the rich) – and certainly not the English themselves, only the "great, splendid, faithful, common people," in other words, only the true Irish. The true Irish, like the true messiah, are defined by suffering, the suffering of the righteous, the suffering of those who have travelled and continue to travel the Irish *via dolorosa* – the "dumb multitudinous throng which sorrowed during the penal night, which bled in '98, which starved in the Famine . . . "[3] No suffering compares to Irish suffering except, of course, the suffering of Christ himself, for Pearse, like Adam Mickiewicz, drew his inspiration from the Catholic wellspring of his youth, mingling his two loves, his church and his nation. How easily, therefore, the passion of Christ merged with the Irish passion in his rhapsodic mind, a mind nourished by his boyhood teachers, the Christian Brothers, as well as by an older generation of literary nationalists such as the political journalist A. M. Sullivan, for whom Irish pain was incomparably greater than the pain and oppression endured by any other nation on earth.[4] Only one earthly contrast was allowed. "Except for the Jews," in the words of a nationalist scribe, no people has "so suffered without dying."[5] Ireland alone, according to Paul Cullen, a cardinal-archbishop of Dublin, can claim the "proud title of the martyr nation of Christ."[6] How easily, therefore, according to a twentieth-century Irish historian,[7] Pearse's obsession with the blood sacrifice of Christ became the model for another blood sacrifice, one which would save Ireland as Christ had saved the world.

For Ireland must and will be saved; its salvation, moreover, must and will be bloody, indeed, a veritable crown of real thorns such as the crown of thorns pressed on the head of Jesus by Roman soldiers, whose part imperial Britain was destined to play in the Irish salvation drama. "As it took the blood of the Son of Man to redeem the world," the schoolmaster declared in a speech to his students at St. Enda's, "so it would take the blood of Irishmen to redeem Ireland."[8] The great Irish poet William Butler Yeats, a nationalist himself who once refused a British knighthood, immortalized this strange fusion of religious martyrdom and political soteriology:

> But Patrick Pearse has said
> In every generation
> Must Ireland's blood be shed.[9]

Must Ireland's blood be shed! – Irish blood, but especially the blood of one Irishman, Pearse himself, described by one of his contemporaries as a "sentimental egotist"[10] who cast his life in a messianic mould and envisaged his death as the culmination of a series of prior immolations in Irish history: the martyrs and prophets of old. One martyrdom in particular, the execution of Robert Emmet in 1803, stirred his patriotic emotions. Emmet (1778–1803), a young man smitten with republican ideas, led a failed uprising against British rule and died on the gallows for high treason. A "dark fascination" soon encircled his fate, turning it into the stuff of legend and the "boy revolutionary" into a popular nationalist icon.[11]

Bold Robert Emmet, the darling of Erin
    Bold Robert Emmet will die with a smile;
Farewell! companions both loyal and daring,
    I will lay down my life for the Emerald Isle.[12]

Glorified by the romantics, especially the lyric poet Thomas Moore, the darling of Erin was idealized beyond all recognition in Irish hagiography during the nineteenth century. Emmet, like the legendary Irish hero Cú Chulainn, died in his youth laughing at death, a defiant gesture in the true Irish tradition. Thus he managed to embody the "sublime and atmospheric" motif of noble death and noble failure found in old Gaelic thought,[13] already saturated with what Matthew Arnold once described as Celtic "sweetness and light, mist and faery magic."[14] A type of Byronic hero and like Lord Byron also a poet, Emmet died the perfect poetic death in the eyes of the adoring nationalist community; the age demanded no less.

Pearse did not invent the heroic theme, but he was not slow to embroider it, infusing his predecessor's demise with the same christological significance that he read into his own life. This was not too difficult because in a prison writing Emmet himself had actually invited his followers to compare his arrest and incarceration as well as his impending doom with the arrest, incarceration and death of Christ.[15] Moreover, elements of Catholic passion mysticism, especially a morbid interest in the wounds of the dying Jesus, began to colour popular descriptions of the patriot's execution soon after it occurred, even though their subject had been a Protestant.[16] Pearse simply made the equation explicit. Emmet was no ordinary political victim; Emmet, whose mortal end as well as his life was nothing less than Christlike "in its perfection"; Emmet, who died with "laughing lips" as Cú Chulainn had died with laughing lips (did Jesus die with laughing lips?); Emmet, whose death was fraught with redemptive meaning and power, at least for the Irish people.[17] Indeed, the redemptive death of Emmet seemed to ignite a similar dream in Pearse, who also contrived to die as he believed Emmet had died, a pure sacrificial lamb at brutish alien hands for the sake of the Christ-nation, the Irish race.

This at any rate was how the schoolmaster of St. Enda's saw himself, a Christ-figure and a personification of Ireland, the innocent and holy land crucified as Christ was crucified and as the poet-dramatist-polemicist (Pearse was all three) would soon be crucified. In his patriotic play *An Rí* (The King), performed in Dublin in 1913, a saintly and Christlike youth Giolla na Naomh dies on the battlefield in order to save his people, clearly a prototype of the playwright himself both in his innocence and in the nature of his death.[18] From such bloody atonements – blood, real blood, was always essential – a "new Ireland, resurrected, pure, Gaelic and Catholic, unspoiled by England and the modern age" would by divine fiat arise "triumphant over its eternal enemy, Protestant materialistic England."[19] It was only fitting, therefore, for Pearse to plot an insurrection against British rule, choosing – again, it was only fitting – Easter Monday, the Christian feast of the resurrection, for his uprising; the symbolism was of consummate importance. What transpired is easily described. The self-anointed Irish messiah and several hundred co-rebels from the Irish National Volunteers armed themselves and seized strategic positions in downtown Dublin, including the general post office, on April 24, 1916 and proclaimed Irish independence, naming their youthful leader president of the provisional government of the Irish republic. Alas, the new republic was short-lived; however, it was expected, even meant, to be short-lived, for its true intent was a crypto-Catholic "national Passion Play," at least in the mind of its instigator.[20]

Whether all of his fellow Sinn Fein (Ourselves Alone) insurrectionists saw the melodrama in the same light is perhaps another question. By Saturday the revolution was over. The British, at war with Germany and fearful of German interference (in fact, Sinn Fein courted German help and Sir Roger Casement, another anti-British militant, landed on the Irish coast on April 20 from a German submarine), were in no mood for seditious antics on what was still British soil. Because of the harsh climate of wartime, the British commanding officer Sir John Maxwell reacted in a draconian fashion, and harsh penalties ensued; Pearse, Casement and a number of other insurgents were summarily executed, a political–military blunder of the first magnitude. To shoot the Easter rebels, as George Bernard Shaw warned at the time, was to canonize them.[21] Nationalist fires were freshly stoked, and the innocuous and, until his death, not especially popular Patrick Pearse found the posthumous niche he had so fervently craved in the pantheon of national saints and martyrs[22] Had he not been executed, the consequences might have been less grave. As another icon of the outraged Irish, his ghost helped to turn Catholic opinion in a republican direction, although other factors assisted this shift. A near fatal blow was inflicted on the cause of moderation, badly damaging both the politics of constitutional nationalism and the Irish Parliamentary Party led by John Redmond (1879–1918), the champion of compromise and Anglo-Irish reconciliation.[23]

Pearse has been described as a soft and gentle man, a pious devotee of the Virgin Mary, a "schoolmaster of Ireland," a man who would never have injured a child or an animal,[24] an apostle of love, as indeed he was; his love, however, was for the Irish – the true Irish – alone. Toward Ireland's enemies, his sentiments were decidedly less Christlike, as one ordinarily understands the term, in fact completely fanatical, involving murder, religiously sanctified murder. The sanctification rested on a literal rather than a metaphorical reading of the gospel text that Jesus came not to bring peace but a sword.[25] Thus Pearse's 'holy nationalism,' to cite Conor Cruise O'Brien,[26] spawned a doctrine of holy violence, ultimately "the violence of pagan heroic Ireland,"[27] a pre-Christian Celtic ferocity wedded to Christian ideals and symbols, thereby standing them on their head. Love signified hatred in the mind of the mild and gentle Pearse, that is to say, love and hatred were naturally and properly conjoined: to love the Irish is to hate the English and their pseudo-Irish lackeys (later this came to mean the Protestants of Northern Ireland). He saw no moral contradiction. His holy nationalism, of course, was also a republican nationalism in the spirit of Emmet and others who drew their models from the radical egalitarianism of the American and French republics. He was neither the first nor the last of the Irish martyr-saviours, although his execution was probably the most efficacious of the political deaths in modern Irish history. It left Catholics and Protestants deeply divided – even the most nationalistic Protestants did not regard Pearse as a Christ-figure – and planted the seed of new troubles, which were not long in coming.

They came in 1918 when, also unwisely, the British government of David Lloyd George threatened to impose conscription on Ireland, propelling even more of the Catholic populace into the arms of Sinn Fein, the party that saw itself as the incarnate soul of the nation.[28] It was then led by Eamon de Valera. Moderate nationalism largely collapsed, all attempts to forge a solution to the now explosive Irish problem also collapsed, sabotaged by the darkening mood in the country and the growing polarization between its various factions. The result was a Sinn Fein victory over the Irish Parliamentary Party in the British general election in December, 1918.★ Refusing to sit in the House of Commons, the Sinn Fein victors established an extra-legal parliament of their own in Dublin, the Dáil Eireann (January 21, 1919) and issued another declaration of independence. Suppression and violence followed, including terrorist acts against the Royal Irish Constabulary and retaliatory acts against the insurrectionists by the pro-British counter-insurgency 'Black and Tans,' causing Ireland to sink into anarchy and

★ However, a vote for Sinn Fein did not necessarily signify a vote for war with Britain.

civil war. On December 23, 1920, as a desperate measure, the British parliament partitioned Ireland, separating the mostly Protestant north from the mostly Catholic south, a split accepted by the north but rejected by the south until 1922 when the Dáil settled for southern autonomy in the form of the Irish Free State. De Valera and his republican followers, however, refused to endorse the settlement negotiated by Michael Collins and Arthur Griffith, pitting nationalist against nationalist and plunging the country into a fresh spate of murders, including that of Collins himself. Once unleashed, the dogs of war are not easily restrained. Having survived his fluctuating fortunes, and having broken with Sinn Fein to found an even more radical party Fianna Fáil (Soldiers of Destiny), De Valera finally re-entered the Dáil in 1927 to become in the course of time the dominant figure in the new nation-state. Despite his march to power, neither he nor anyone else was able to realize the "glorious and immortal" Ireland envisioned by Pearse, the great "day of the Lord" for which the saints and heroes of the Irish nation shed their precious blood.[29]

The saints and heroes of the past, or, as they have been famously described,[30] the Irish ancestral voices, indeed, the 'living dead' and veritable ghosts of the great ancestors, did not all die as political sacrificial victims, but those who did approximate best the tortured logic of a religiously infused nationalism. Foremost among the living dead along with Emmet are Theobald Wolfe Tone, a suicide in a British prison, the so called Manchester martyrs, and the more recent Bobby Sands, another suicide. Tone (1763–1798), like Emmet a convert to the republican dogmas of the French Revolution, plotted with the French – he actually became an officer in the French army – to overthrow British rule in Ireland by means of an invasion. Once on shore, if all went well, the invaders would be joined by Irish rebels, the self-styled United Irishmen from "Jacobin Belfast" as well as elsewhere, and the two forces together would triumph over the Protestant Ascendancy and cast off British rule. All, however, did not go well; the French armada, like the Spanish armada in 1588, came to grief on the high seas in 1796, a second attempted invasion in 1797 also failed, and the Irish uprising, described by a subsequent nationalist historian as "one of the most glorious chapters in Irish history," was crushed in 1798.[31] Tone fell into British hands and, since the temper of the times did not suffer even treasonable thoughts, soon found himself sentenced to death. However, the rebel cheated the gallows by cutting his own throat first, leaving a posthumous legend that his captors had murdered him in secret. Suicide to avoid being hanged was inconsistent with the concept of noble martyrdom, but self-immolation for national glory was another matter. The latter was sanctified and celebrated by the nationalists in their sorrowful vision of Irish history, a vale of tears that extended back to the Anglo-Norman invasion of 1169 and numerous subsequent infamies, in particular the Tudor plantations and the never forgotten Cromwellian massacres at Drogheda and Wexford (1649).

As happened with Emmet, a Tone cult arose after his death making him one of the illustrious sons of Ireland to be praised and emulated forever by the faithful, of whom Pearse was a pre-eminent example. Although like Emmet a Protestant, Tone had regarded the Irish Protestants who formed the ascendancy as usurpers and therefore not truly Irish.[32] More deistic than orthodox in his religious convictions (another sign of French influence), he came to believe nevertheless in the quasi-Catholic sanctity of blood sacrifice and its quasi-philosophical notion of victory in defeat.[33] In this respect, he was again similar to Emmet. Both men were sons of the Enlightenment in their republican ardour; both men were also creatures of the romantic age in their half mystical, half tribal sense of Irish nationhood, a view of things fully in keeping with the prevalent mood in European art, music and letters at the time. Their nationalist canonization fertilized the cultural soil for more holy martyrs as political radicalism reappeared during the terrible famine of the 1840s, resulting in the birth of new revolutionary movements such as the Young Ireland Party (1840) and the paramilitary Irish Revolutionary (Fenian) Brotherhood (1858), a secretive organization modelled on the Italian Carbonari. It is noteworthy that Thomas Davis (1814–1845), the poet-intellectual whose desire to foster a Gaelic-Celtic national ethos helped to inspire the Young Ireland Party, was himself inspired by the philosophical writings of Johann-Gottfried Herder.[34]

An abortive uprising organized by the Young Irelanders in Tipperary in 1848 produced no new Tones or Emmets but probably served to increase the disaffection of the radical element in the general populace. A second larger uprising organized by the more militant Fenians in 1867 also failed, but on this occasion the blood of war was not spilled in vain. Three young Fenian Irishmen were executed in Manchester, England, for the murder of a police guard at a time when public executions were still staged. They were not involved in the Fenian insurrection but this did not prevent their immediate beatification in Ireland where in their innocence and nobility of character they were compared to Christ, dying "as He who walked and taught, by the sad inland lakes of Palestine."[35] The lurid contrast between the pure-hearted 'Manchester martyrs,'

Allen, Larkin and O'Brien, and the cruel English mob that, according to
the pro-Fenian press, jeered at their sufferings with "ribald" laughs overwhelmed Irish sensibilities; the pious were reminded not only of the
saviour himself but also of the Christian innocents murdered by the
Romans, the martyrs of antiquity. Mock funerals and funeral processions
were staged in Irish cities, and the graves of the executed Fenians began
to attract pilgrims from Irish communities even in foreign lands. Suddenly
the roster of slaughtered saints acquired three new recruits, and the
nationalist bards were not slow to pen their praise.

> Upon the scaffold grim they died, the last in Erin's cause
> Upon the gallows high they swung, by England's bloodstained laws;
> Like Emmet, Sheares, Fitzgerald, Tone, and hundreds true and bold
> They died to make their native land a nation as of old.[36]

Was Ireland, as has been suggested, starting to develop a funerary culture
(*theatrum mortis* or the theatre of the dead)?[37] If so, it had many celebrants.
Only a short time prior to the Manchester martyrs, huge crowds in New
York and Dublin had swarmed to public rites attending the re-interment
on Irish soil of the mortal remains of Terence McManus, a Young
Irelander who had died in 1861 in San Francisco: a massive and cleverly
orchestrated Fenian propaganda feat that made no small impact on a
sympathetic America.

One famous muse of the Irish Christ-nation was "Ireland's Joan of
Arc,"[38] the beautiful English-born actress Maud Gonne (1866–1953),
beloved of Yeats and the subject of some of his poems. An intensely
romantic woman and a Catholic convert because of the supposed inner
fusion between Catholicism and the Irish soul, she once played the title
role in Yeats' political play *Cathleen ni Houlihan* at the Abbey Theatre in
Dublin in 1902. Set on Irish soil during the 1798 uprising, the melodrama
pulsates with revolutionary zeal; Cathleen, of course, personifies Ireland,
crucified by England, but in spite of this fact "a young girl with the walk
of a queen" – the "image of a free and independent nation."[39] The young
girl with the walk of a queen, however, was old as well as young, a
complex figure with powerful roots in Celtic mythology, the "fierce
virgin of a religion much older than Christianity," indeed the goddess of
an ancient folkloric cult, the 'old woman' of Ireland deprived of her
land.[40] *Cathleen ni Houlihan* has been described as the most powerful piece
of nationalist propaganda ever composed.[41]

Later Gonne had religious visions. Once, while attending Mass, her
mind focused on its sacrificial essence, she saw dancing before her eyes

the spirits of dead Irishmen, causing her to reflect on their deaths in light of the great heavenly sacrifice. Many of the dancing spirits had perished as British soldiers during the European war (this was 1915); their deaths were misplaced and their fate was tragic but she knew that their souls would rejoin the "spiritual Ireland" in which she fervently believed.★ Others had died for Ireland itself, bestowing on their deaths a higher and deeper meaning. They died, Gonne writes, "with a definite idea of sacrifice to an ideal . . . leading in wonderful patterns to a deeper peace, the peace of the Crucified, which is above the currents of nationalities & storms, but . . . they will not be separated from Ireland for as an entity she has followed the path of Sacrifice & tasted of the Grail . . . "[42] Holy Ireland, the Christ-nation, mystically and romantically conceived, affixed to the Catholic Mass, finds here its most fanciful delineation.

Yeats, who had aspired to become an Irish Victor Hugo, grew less certain.[43] The "terrible beauty" that was born on Easter, 1916, seems to have filled him with disquiet.

Too long a sacrifice
can make a stone of the heart.†

The nationalist poet had ample reason for his uneasiness, probably guessing that more martyrdoms lay ahead. If so, he was correct. Most recent in time and most in the classical self-immolation mode was the death of another young revolutionary poet, Bobby Sands, in a Northern Irish prison in 1981. A combatant in the Irish Republican Army, Sands was arrested and imprisoned for the illegal possession of arms in order to inflict harm following a bombing episode and gun battle in Belfast in 1976. His imprisonment, according to the nationalist constituency, was nothing less than a prolonged *via dolorosa*, another Calvary, for he was destined to die "cruelly murdered by the British government," indeed

---

★ There is a hint of theosophy in Gonne's vision. Madam Blavatsky (1831–91) attracted a considerable following among the mystically inclined of the later nineteenth and early twentieth centuries.

† I write it out in verse –
MacDonagh and MacBride
And Connolly and Pearse
Now and in time to be,
Wherever green is worn,
Are changed, changed utterly:
A terrible beauty is born.

Easter 1916

crucified as still another personification of the "true Irish nation" – meaning, of course, the Catholic Irish.[44] In actual fact, the idealized Sands died as a result of a hunger strike because the prison authorities refused to allow him to wear civilian clothes: a concession that, if granted – so it was argued – would have changed his status to that of political prisoner. Had he won this cherished propaganda victory, he might not have starved himself, although this is uncertain; death by starvation was already a rebel tradition.[45] What is certain, however, is that the youthful republican poet, who attended Mass in prison (partly to break the monotony), cast both his person and his cause, his life and his anticipated death, in the same sacred matrix as his Pearsean model, merging his body with the "mystical body of the Republican movement" as well as the mystical body of Christ:[46]

> The beady eyes they peered at me
> The time had come to be,
> To walk the lonely road
> Like that of Calvary.
> And take up the cross of Irishmen
> Who've carried liberty.[47]

Unlike the dying Jesus in the New Testament, however, neither forgiveness of his crucifiers nor any hint of such softens the martyr's final words; only hatred emanates from his prison verse. So resonant was the chord struck by his plight among angry and alienated Catholics in Northern Ireland that, shortly before his death on the cross (so to speak), the new nationalist saint was elected to the House of Commons from his prison cell in a gesture of defiance. Since republican victors were not expected to take their seats in any case, the state of the candidate's health was not an issue.

Despite his popularity and fateful death, neither Sands nor his martyr-predecessors represented the wider stream of Irish nationalism, although the ancestral voices that whispered their sanguinary counsels from the grave were by no means peripheral. However, the pathological nature of the blood sacrifice tradition was always offensive to nationalists of a more temperate disposition, especially those who sought a constitutional solution to Ireland's woes. Violence was disavowed by such central personages in the long slow struggle for Irish freedom as Daniel O'Connell (1775–1847) and Charles Stewart Parnell (1846–1891), Ireland's so called "uncrowned kings," as well as by the more prosaic John Redmond, Parnell's successor in the House of Commons.

To the eloquent O'Connell, a Catholic and the father of Catholic emancipation,* (footnote on p. 77) the Irish nation signified all of the inhabitants of Ireland, not merely Catholics,[48] although in secret the great Liberator seems to have harboured some anti-Protestant as well as 'anti-Saxon' (i.e., anti-English) sentiments.[49] Nonetheless O'Connell sought the peaceful repeal of the union between Ireland and Britain while still retaining an essential political connection. He was not a republican. To the more equivocal Parnell, a Protestant and the apostle of home rule (the effective repeal of the union), the Irish nation also signified all the inhabitants of Ireland, or he would have disqualified himself. An able parliamentarian, respected by Gladstone, he possessed the classic attributes of the political classes, in particular the juggling skills required to achieve difficult political goals. Perhaps for this reason, his true feelings remain a matter of some conjecture to historians. A veritable master of imprecision, he flirted with the militant Fenians by supporting the radical John Mitchel in an 1875 by-election and praising the "pale-faced martyr Emmet" in one of his speeches. However, he refused to join them, or so it is believed.[50] Ambiguity rather than zealotry was his trademark, nor was murder to his taste. It is alleged that his face turned ashen on learning of the brutal assassination of the new chief secretary for Ireland Lord Frederick Cavendish and his (Irish Catholic) undersecretary by ex-Fenians in Dublin in May, 1882: the notorious Phoenix Park murders.[51] If so, the fact is revealing.

Ulster

If Catholic Irish nationalism of the radical Pearsean strain poured its passions into the motif of crucifixion by Protestant England, Protestant Irish nationalism discovered its own mythological core in a counter-crucifixion: the Catholic oppression of the Irish Protestants, beginning with the well-attested massacre of thousands of Ulster settlers by Catholic insurgents in 1641.[52] Thereafter the Protestant memory became suffused with images of victimization, a view greatly reinforced after the siege of Derry in 1688 by the Catholic king James II. Like parallel traumas in Irish Catholic sacred history, the assault on Derry became an axial event in Ulster Protestant sacred history, a type of collective murder or attempted murder of the Protestant faithful by the forces of evil associated with the Roman papacy. Time, as time always does, soon turned the heroism of the Protestant defenders into a panegyric. The fabled thirteen apprentice

---

* The Catholic Emancipation Bill was passed by the British Parliament in 1829.

boys who barred the gates of the city against the Catholic army evolved into iconic heroes, and the siege itself with its attendant ordeals became a paradigm of defiance, solidarity and sacrifice, similar to the travails of the biblical children of Israel at the hands of their Egyptian, Assyrian and Babylonian foes.[53] When the siege was broken by the Protestant king William III in 1689, it was likened to the deliverance of the ancient people of God from the bondage of Pharoah. Dare one also call it a resurrection? Certainly the final defeat of the Catholic monarch by his Protestant son-in-law at the Battle of the Boyne in 1690 was transfused with religious overtones. God had vindicated the righteous. The Ulster Protestants, especially the Old Testament-oriented Presbyterians, were fond of biblical analogies and strongly attracted to notions of divine election.[54] As Protestants of a Calvinist bent they were naturally predisposed to interpret their history in a biblical frame while identifying their cause and thus themselves with the elect people of God and the crucified Son of God.[55] In this way, they managed to place their community firmly on the side of everlasting goodness.

This singular compound of faith and politics, while never universal in Ulster (it was weaker among Anglicans and Methodists), was strong enough to permeate loyalist thought for centuries. It rose to the fore in modern times when Catholic militancy increased and when tensions mounted surrounding the prospect of home rule among supporters of the 1801 union. As agitation for political change grew stronger, the reaction against political change also grew stronger, and all of Protestant-dominated Ulster, metaphorically speaking, began at a certain point to shut its gates, replaying on a larger scale the old siege of Derry.[56] Derry (or Londonderry, depending on one's political sympathies) acquired virtually the status of a holy city in Protestant-loyalist eyes, being both a place and a "state of mind."[57] To Lord Macaulay, the wall of Londonderry was to the Ulster Protestants "what the trophy of Marathon was to the Athenians":[58] a glorious monument to British liberty as well as Protestant freedom, those twin spirits of the dawning age of Anglo Saxon global triumph. The original apprentice boys no more than the Athenian warriors of old understood their act of defiance as a great moment in the eternal struggle against tyranny, whether ancient or modern, whether Persian or papal. If the Protestant ascendancy in Ireland developed a siege mentality after a fierce struggle with the Catholic Jacobites,★ its fears were mitigated by the conviction that providence was on their side and that God was their protector. The Orange Order and the Apprentice Boys

★ The supporters of King James II and his Stuart heirs after the loss of his throne.

clubs became the special champions of this half political, half religious vision.

As Catholic Ireland had its liberator in O'Connell and its uncrowned kings in O'Connell and Parnell, Protestant Ireland, or to be more exact, Protestant Ulster, had both its liberator and its uncrowned king in the person of Sir Edward Carson (1854–1935). This is slightly ironic because Carson, the "generalissmo" of Ulster unionism,[59] was neither from Ulster nor, for that matter, a covenant-minded Presbyterian, but a native of Dublin and a member of the Church of Ireland. One of the most eminent barristers of his day – he defended the Marquess of Queensbury against the libel charge brought by Oscar Wilde – and First Lord of the Admiralty in the cabinet of David Lloyd George, he was also in his own way an ardent Irish patriot who sincerely believed that union with Britain was in the best interests of his country. So strong was this belief that his campaign against home rule assumed the character of a religious crusade and even at one point threatened armed rebellion against the British state should this hated measure ever be imposed on its Irish citizenry.[60] The threat was not idle; armaments were secretly imported from Germany in defiance of the cabinet. When, on September 28, 1912 ('Ulster Day'), the Solemn League and Covenant was signed in the Belfast City Hall by Irish loyalists determined to defend Ulster against the "calamity" of a national parliament on Irish soil, the great Dublin lawyer was the first to affix his signature: over 470,000 names, both men and women, followed, although the latter actually signed a parallel declaration.[61] God, the covenant proclaims, will surely defend the Protestant cause.[62]

The eruption of war on the continent in 1914 saved Carson and the Ulster Volunteers from the necessity of rebellion and thus Ireland from civil strife, at least for the moment. In the event of such a conflict, a "glorious self-immolation," indeed, a "Unionist blood-sacrifice" was envisaged: in other words, not defeat but crucifixion and martyrdom.[63] In an unanticipated turn of fate, a veritable Unionist blood sacrifice did in fact take place during the Battle of the Somme (1916), especially on the terrible first day (July 1) when the Thirty-Sixth Ulster Division was decimated along with scores of other British troops, including, incidentally, many Irish Catholic soldiers, a loss never forgotten by Irish Protestants and one instantly associated with 1641 and 1688.* Coincidence sometimes plays a strange role in human affairs; the Battle

---

* The annual Orange march with fife and drum at Drumcree in County Armagh is a commemoration of the first day of the Battle of the Somme.

79

of the Boyne was also fought on July 1, although it is commemorated for calendar reasons on July 12.

> God in heaven, if you hear the words of man, I speak to you this day. I do it now to ask we be spared. I do it to ask for strength. Strength for these men around me, strength for myself. If you are a just and merciful God, show your mercy this day. Save us. Save our country. Destroy our enemies at home and on this field of battle. Lest this day at the Somme be as glorious in the memory of Ulster as that day at the Boyne, when you scattered our enemies. Lead us back for this exile. To Derry, to the Foyle. To Belfast and the Langan. To Armagh. To Tyrone. To the Bann and its banks. To Erne and its islands. Protect them. Protect us. Protect me. Let us fight bravely. Let us win gloriously. Lord, look down on us . . . Observe the sons of Ulster marching towards the Somme. I love their lives. I love my own life. I love my home. I love my Ulster. Ulster. Ulster. Ulster. Ulster. Ulster. Ulster. Ulster. Ulster.[64]

This "quixotic" speech from a 1985 play by the Irish playwright Frank McGuinness is delivered by the central character on the eve of battle in order to remind the British Ulster division as they fixed their bayonets that the real battle was for their homeland, joining the French river to the Irish river, the Somme to the Boyne, that great "river of mythic significance" in the Protestant folk memory.[65] The actual battle, of course, was anything but a triumph as far as the Ulster division was concerned, but, as in Irish Catholic iconography, defeat signifies victory, the paradoxical victory of the martyred righteous.[66]

> Life? – 'twas a little thing to give:
> > Death? –'twas a toy to try.
> They knew that Ulster dared not live,
> > Did they not dare to die.[67]

So wrote the Protestant poet F. S. Boas. Even the Catholic Francis Ledwidge, the only true Irish poet of the battlefield comparable to the great English war poets Wilfred Owen and Siegfried Sassoon, elevated the Irish sacrificial spirit during the First World War to an irresistible religious plane, choosing as his proof-text another military fiasco, the failed Gallipoli campaign (1915–16):

> Who said that such an emprise could be vain?
> Were they not one with Christ Who strove and died?

Let Ireland weep but not for sorrow. Weep
That by her sons a land is sanctified
For Christ Arisen, and angels once again
Come back like exile birds to guard their sleep.[68]

The poet, who, despite his British uniform, was in his heart of hearts sympathetic to the Easter uprising, had a different patriotism in mind than that of Ulster Protestantism, but it was scarcely possible to glorify Irish soldiers in the British army without embracing the Protestant dead as noble martyrs as well, at least implicitly. Nor would the Ulster Protestants have rejected the beatific ascription, although they manifestly did not regard their Catholic fellow countrymen in the same christological light. Easily ignored or forgotten was the fact that the crucified Thirty-Sixth Ulster Division contained Catholic soldiers as well.

The crucifixion and martyrdom of the Somme was certainly real enough, but the anticipated Protestant crucifixion and martyrdom at Catholic hands never transpired, although its expectation never vanished. Nor, for that matter, has the curious paradox that lies at the heart of Ulster Protestant nationalism, which is more accurately described as a "quasi" or "embryonic" nationalism,[69] disappeared from the Loyalist constituency: a determination, if the worst should ever come to the worst, to resist the British in order to preserve the union with Britain. After he died, Carson, by then Lord Carson, who had never desired or sought the partition of Ireland, became enshrined despite this fact as a Protestant Moses who had led the chosen people to a promised land, saving them from the Catholic pharaoh (the pope) and his minions in the south.[70] His name is still revered in ultra-loyalist circles, notably the Orange Lodge, so long the dominant influence in the new Protestant ascendancy of the north. The ascendancy retained its dominance for another generation or two, but proved too intransigent to accommodate reform when the need for reform became painfully obvious during the mounting turbulence of the late 1960s. Yet one unionist was able to read the signs of the times, namely Terence O'Neill, the fourth prime minister of Northern Ireland. In contrast to most of his Protestant compatriots, O'Neill sought to treat the Catholic minority with "due kindness and consideration," wooing and winning their allegiance by this gentle means.[71] His 'positive unionism,' however, so inflamed the loyalist hard core that the banners of Protestant defiance were raised against him: once more on Irish soil Protestant liberty saw itself encircled and besieged by Catholic tyranny![72] To the Ulster Catholics, on the other hand, tyranny possessed a different face. They raised the banner of civil rights, the international *cause célèbre* of the decade, and a violent clash between the two alienated and polarized communities began to loom.

It happened in 1968 and 1969. Mob violence in (London) Derry and Belfast involving both Protestants and Catholics produced an escalating crisis that effectively doomed Stormont, the seat of Protestant rule, as well as O'Neill himself, who was forced from office by angry factions within his own party. When the Stormont parliament was finally swept away by the British government in 1972, the Protestant establishment was left without the means of coercion that its political dynasties had formerly enjoyed. What had been removed could not be restored, at least in its old form; Northern Ireland became a subsidiary of the British state, ruled directly from London. A long period of troubles ensued during which a new Protestant knight-errant appeared in Ulster politics, the charismatic and demagogic Ian Paisley (1926–), a fundamentalist preacher and the founder of the schismatic Free Presbyterian Church. It was Paisley who made himself O'Neill's *bête noire* by opposing even minor concessions to the Ulster Catholics, employing classic harassment tactics and on one infamous occasion allowing his followers to hurl abuse at "apostate" dignitaries attending the general assembly of the mainstream Presbyterian Church (1966), including even Lord Erskine, the governor of Northern Ireland and proxy of the Queen.[73]

Imprisonment for instigating a riot only served to magnify his stature among disaffected Protestants, bestowing a faint aura of possible martyrdom – one is reminded of Bobby Sands★ – although, in fact, his term was of short duration (three months). So also was a second prison term in 1969. Following his second release, the preacher turned increasingly to the political arena, winning a seat in the Stormont parliament in 1970 and the British House of Commons scarcely two months later. Thus emboldened, Paisley played an instrumental role in creating another schism, this time within unionism itself, forming with others the ultra-loyalist Democratic Unionist Party in 1971. As "unwavering sentinels" of the true political and religious bastion, its adherents saw themselves as engaged in a "last battle for Ulster,"[74] a faithful remnant fearful of both republican domination and betrayal by perfidious Albion and hence determined not to yield a single inch. Unionism was thus divided into various factions. At first only a sectarian movement, Paisleyism spread as the troubles deepened, beginning with 'Bloody Sunday' (January 30, 1972), the inadvertent deaths of thirteen Catholics at military hands

---

★ It is of more than marginal interest that Paisley's Belfast church is called the Martyr's Memorial Church.

during a banned march that ended in confrontation and disaster. In the course of time the Democratic Unionist Party became the largest political party in Northern Ireland, overtaking the less doctrinaire Ulster Unionist Party. It retains this status today, although even more intransigent parties now outflank it.

As Paisley strode the stage like a colossus, periodic attempts were made to design a new mode of governance based on a division of power between the two warring communities. No consensus was reached, however, despite constitutional forums and conferences, British–Irish consultations, new assemblies, new elections, new initiatives and new cease-fires; in the end, communal fear and distrust proved too strong. Nor did the Anglo-Irish Agreement signed in 1985 by Britain and the Irish Republic, allowing the Irish government a voice in the affairs of the province, yield the desired fruit, since it was bitterly opposed by Sinn Fein on the one side and most unionists on the other side. It was seen as a betrayal and greeted with fury. The Protestant cup of wrath overflowed when further martyrdoms occurred at Enniskillen during Remembrance Day ceremonies (November 8, 1987) and Omagh (August 16, 1998), martyrdoms readily linked to the Somme and the Boyne by what has been called the 'politics of remembrance.'[75] These atrocities, however, the work of republican extremists, outraged Catholic as well as Protestant opinion in both Irelands, the first sign of incipient change. An extraordinary act of personal forgiveness, moreover, arising from the 'Poppy Day' massacre at Enniskillen, helped to soften Catholic and Protestant hearts.*

Despite Paisley and the Paisleyites, despite the cycle of violence, Ulster Protestantism underwent its own subtle transformation. The Solemn Covenant that had united the northern loyalists in a great ecstatic moment in 1912 began to lose some of its transcendent authority. Among the churches, a mood of disquiet unsettled the truisms that had informed such men as Lord Craigavon and Lord Brookeborough, the political heirs and successors of Lord Carson. Not all Protestants, of course, and certainly not all Presbyterians were prepared to surrender their deeply held convictions; "holy fragments" clung to the true faith.[76] These holy fragments kept alive the holy war, assisted by paramilitary organizations such as the Ulster Defence Association (UDA) and the Ulster Volunteer Force (UVF) spawned on the backstreets: in other words, the proverbial mob spoiling for a fight in any social order afflicted with serious tensions.

---

* On the part of a man named Gordon Wilson, whose daughter Marie died in the explosion. He forgave her IRA killers.

Such mobs ultimately care less about ideas than about acting out the accumulated resentment and fury of a disadvantaged and threatened underclass. In this respect, the hardened ultra-loyalist UDA and UVF recruits and the hardened ultra–republican IRA recruits (such as Bobby Sands) were much alike.

The true faith lives on, although a more peaceful climate has now settled on the British province. In the wake of political reforms, the Irish Republican Army has surrendered its arms and Sinn Fein has consented to support the Northern Irish police. New elections (March 2007) have produced a new assembly and new hopes. Even Paisley seems to have mellowed, and, in a curious turn of events, has in his old age actually become the first minister of a reconstituted Catholic-Protestant jurisdiction.★ Yet Protestant religious nationalism like Catholic religious nationalism remains as a haunting presence, even if its Demosthenes has tempered his orations with pragmatism and perhaps also the sweet savour of power.[77] It is difficult to forget his sermon against Margaret Thatcher for having committed an unpardonable sin in signing the Anglo-Irish Agreement in 1985. After handing the British prime minister over to the devil in a prayer,[78] the preacher–politician, then a figure reminiscent of the fanatical Scottish covenanters famously depicted in Sir Walter Scott's novel *Old Mortality*, uttered these words:

> God has a people in this province. There are more born-again people in Ulster to the square mile than anywhere else in the world. This little province has had the peculiar preservation of divine Providence. You only have to read the history of Ulster to see that time after time when it seemed humanly impossible to extricate Ulster from seeming disaster, that God intervened. Why? God has a purpose for this province, and this plant of Protestantism sown here in the north-eastern part of this island. The enemy has tried to root it out, but it still grows today, and I believe, like a grain of mustard seed, its future is going to be mightier yet. God Who made her mighty will make her mightier yet in His Divine will.[79]

Notes

1   P. H. Pearse, *The Sovereign People*, Dublin: Whelan and Son, 1916, pp. 7–8.
2   Emmanuel Joseph Sieyès, *Qu'est ce-que le Tiers État?*, 1789.
3   Ibid., pp. 5, 7
4   As cited in R. F. Foster, *The Irish Story: Telling Tales and Making it Up in Ireland*, London: Penguin Press, 2001, p. 8.

★ Following the March elections, Paisley and Gerry Adams of Sinn Fein held an unprecedented meeting in which the leaders of the two diametrically opposed factions agreed to share power.

5 Cited in Liam Kennedy, *Colonialism, Religion and Nationalism in Ireland*, Belfast: Institute of Irish Studies, 1996, p. 182.

6 Cited in Brian Jenkins, *Irish Nationalism and the British State: From Repeal to Revolutionary Nationalism*, Kingston & Montreal: McGill–Queen's University Press, 2006, p. 106.

7 Xavier Carty, *In Bloody Protest – The Tragedy of Patrick Pearse*, Dublin: Able Press, 1978, p. 61.

8 Cited in William Irwin Thompson, *The Imagination of an Insurrection: A study of an Ideological Movement*, West Stockbridge, Mass.: Lindisfarne Press, 1982, p. 89.

9 W. B. Yeats, "Three Songs to the One Burden"

10 Cited in Ruth Dudley Edwards, *Patrick Pearse: The Triumph* of Failure, London: Faber & Faber, 1977, p. 337.

11 Cf. Marianne Elliott, *Robert Emmet: The making of a Legend*, London: Profile Books, 2003, pp. 5, 181.

12 "The Last Moments of Robert Emmet" (anonymous, circa 1900).

13 Ibid., p. 113.

14 Thompson, op. cit., p. 15.

15 Elliott, op. cit., p 88.

16 Ibid., p. 151.

17 Pearse delivered two speeches before Irish American audiences at the Emmet Commemoration in the Academy of Music, Brooklyn, New York, in March, 1914. Cf. Elliott, op. cit., pp. 154–155.

18 Cf. Raymond J. Porter, *P. H. Pearse*, New York: Twayne Publishers, 1973, pp. 100–101.

19 Seán Farrell Moran, "Patrick Pearse and Patriotic Soteriology: The Irish Republican Tradition and the Sanctification of Political Self-Immolation," *The Irish Terrorism Experience*, Yonah Alexander & Alan O'Day (editors), Dartmouth: Dartmouth Publishing Co., 1991, p. 17.

20 Conor Cruise O'Brien, *Ancestral Voices: Religion and Nationalism in Ireland*, Chicago: University of Chicago Press, 1995, p. 108.

21 Cf. *The Gonne-Yeats Letters*, Anna MacBride & A. Norman Jeffares (editors), London: Hutchinson, 1992, p. 377.

22 Carty, op. cit., p. 65.

23 See Joseph P. Finnan, *John Redmond and Irish Unity 1912–1918*, Syracuse: Syracuse University Press, 2004, p. 193f.

24 Cited in Edwards, op. cit., p. 336.

25 Carty, op. cit., p. 54.

26 Cf. Conor Cruise O'Brien, *God Land: Reflections on Religion and Nationalism*, Cambridge, Mass.: Harvard University Press, 1988, passim.

27 Patrick O'Farrell, cited in Carty, op. cit., p. 64.

28 Cf. Patrick Maume, *The Long Gestation: Irish Nationalist Life 1891–1918*, New York: St. Martin's Press, 1999, p. 217.

29 Pearse, op. cit., p. 20. It is an interesting and perhaps significant footnote to De Valera's career that on May 3, 1945, in his capacity as Taoiseach (prime

minister) he visited the German legation in Dublin to express his condolences on the death of Adolf Hitler in his bunker in Berlin on April 30.

30   O'Brien, op. cit..

31   C. Desmond Greaves, *Theobald Wolfe Tone and the Irish Nation*, Dublin: Fulcrum Press, 1991, p. 101.

32   Marianne Elliott, *Wolfe Tone: Prophet of Irish Independence*, New Haven: Yale University Press, 1989, p. 310.

33   Ibid., p. 379.

34   Cf. Jenkins, op. cit., p. 64.

35   As cited in Gary Owens, "Constructing the martyrs: the Manchester executions and the nationalist imagination," Lawrence W. McBride (ed.), *Images, Icons and the Irish Nationalist Imagination*, Dublin: Four Courts Press, 1999, p. 22.

36   Ibid. (cited), p. 23.

37   Ibid., p. 25.

38   Cf. Margaret Ward, *Maud Gonne: Ireland's Joan of Arc*, London: Pandora Press, 1990.

39   Samuel Levenson, *Maud Gonne*, New York: Reader's Digest Press, 1976, p. 194

40   Thompson, op. cit., p. 149.

41   Conor Cruise O'Brien, *Ancestral Voices*, p. 61.

42   Letter to Yeats, November 7, 1915 (*The Gonne–Yeats Letters*, p. 363).

43   Levenson, op. cit., p. 58.

44   As cited in John M. Feehan, *Bobby Sands and the Tragedy of Northern Ireland*, Dublin: Mercier Press, 1983, p. 19.

45   Thomas Ashe, a member of the Irish Republican Brotherhood, died following a hunger strike in a Dublin prison in 1917. It is sometimes forgotten that Eamon de Valera and the Irish government later allowed IRA militants to die of self-imposed starvation in Irish prisons in 1932, 1940 and 1946.

46   Padraig O'Malley, *Biting at the Grave: The Irish Hunger Strikes and the Politics of Despair*, Boston: Beacon Press, 1940, p. 57.

47   Diplock Court.

48   Cf. Oliver MacDonagh, *The Emancipist: Daniel O'Connell 1830–47*, New York: St. Martin's Press, 1989, p. 29.

49   Cf. Jenkins, op. cit., pp. 44–46.

50   Robert Kee, *The Laurel and the Ivy: The Story of Charles Stewart Parnell and Irish Nationalism*, London: Hamish Hamilton, 1993, p. 92. Mitchel, incidentally, also saw himself as a Christlike figure because he had once stood in the dock "between a pair of thieves" (Jenkins, op. cit., p. 116). There is some inconclusive evidence that Parnell may in fact have secretly taken the Fenian oath, in spite of all denials. If so, he was a consummate hypocrite. See Patrick Maume, "Parnell and the J.R.B. oath," *Irish Historical Studies* (Vol. xxix/no. 115/May 1995), pp. 363–370.

51 Ibid., p. 439. Parnell's ashen face also may have been caused by a fear of his own assassination at Fenian hands.

52 How many Protestants were really massacred remains open to question. Still, according to Marcus Tanner, Ulster in 1641 was a "scene of frenzied pogroms" not unlike Bosnia in 1992. See Marcus Tanner, *Ireland's Holy Wars: The Struggle for a Nation's Soul 1500–2000*, New Haven: Yale University Press, 2001, pp. 135–136.

53 Cf. Ian McBride, *The Siege of Derry in Ulster Protestant Mythology*, Dublin: Four Courts Press, 1997, pp. 12–13.

54 Donald Harmon Akenson, *God's Peoples: Covenant and Land in South Africa, Israel, and Ulster*, Montreal & Kingston: McGill-Queen's University Press, 1991, p. 119.

55 See Duncan Morrow, "Suffering for Righteousness' Sake: Fundamentalist Protestantism and Ulster Politics, *Who Are 'The People'?: Unionism, Protestantism and Loyalism in Northern Ireland*, Peter Shirlow & Mark McGovern (eds), London: Pluto Press, 1997, pp. 55–71.

56 McBride, op. cit., p. 67.

57 Ibid., pp. 71–72.

58 Thomas Babington Macaulay, *The History of England*, Vol. III, New York: Harper & Brothers, 1856, p. 190. Macaulay also declared that to write of Ireland was to tread on a volcano whose lava was still glowing!

59 Alvin Jackson, *Sir Edward Carson*, Dublin: Historical Association of Ireland, 1993, p. 29.

60 See A. T. Q.Stewart, *Edward Carson*, Dublin: Gill & Macmillan, 1981, pp. 77–79.

61 The Ulster covenant seems to have been inspired by the 1644 Scottish Solemn League and Covenant with its Calvinist overtones. In keeping with Calvin's political ideas, the Scottish Covenanters maintained that loyalty to the sovereign was contractual, a theme transmitted to the much later Ulster loyalists. One feature of Irish 'Orangeism" was its conditional allegiance to the king. The Ulster justification for defiance of the British government, if the worst came to the worst, was that the Protestants represented the only law-abiding people in Ireland in the face of Catholic lawlessness.

   See David Miller, *Queen's Rebels: Ulster Loyalism in Historical Perspective*, Dublin: Gill & Macmillan, 1978, p. 101.

62 The text reads as follows:
   Being convinced in our consciences that Home Rule would be disastrous to the material well-being of Ulster as well as the whole of Ireland, subversive of our civil and religious freedom, destructive of our citizenship and perilous to the unity of the Empire, we, whose names are under-written, men of Ulster, loyal subjects of His Gracious Majesty King George V, humbly relying on the God whom our fathers in days of stress and trial confidently trusted, do hereby pledge ourselves in solemn Covenant throughout this our time of threatened calamity to stand by one another in defending

for ourselves and our children our cherished possession of equal citizenship
in the United Kingdom and in using all means which may be found necessary to defeat the present conspiracy to set up a Home Rule Parliament in
Ireland. And in the event of such a Parliament being forced upon us we
further solemnly and mutually pledge ourselves to refuse to recognize its
authority. In sure confidence that God will defend the right we hereto
subscribe our names. And further, we individually declare that we have not
already signed this Covenant.

The above was signed by me at _____ 'Ulster Day,' Saturday, 28th
September, 1912.

God Save The King.

63 Jackson, op. cit., p. 40.
64 Frank McGuiness, *Observe the Sons of Ulster Marching Towards the Somme*,
    1985, Part IV.
65 Jim Haughey, *The First World War in Irish Poetry*, Lewisburg: Bucknell
    University Press, 2002, p. 44.
66 Ibid., p. 42.
67 Ibid. (cited), p 119.
68 Francis Ledwidge, *The Irish in Gallipoli*, cited by Haughey, Ibid., p. 89.
    University Press, 2000, p. 159.
69 Miller, op. cit., p. 131.
70 Tanner, op. cit., p. 328.
71 Cf. Marc Mulholland, *Northern Ireland at the Crossroads: Ulster Unionism in
    the O'Neill Years 1960–9*, Houndmills, Basingstoke: Macmillan Press, 2000,
    p. 1.
72 Ibid., p. 92. It must be added that the prime minister's somewhat ineffec-
    tual leadership was a factor in the rise of Protestant extremism, notably what
    Mulholland calls the "inflammatory phenomenon of Paisleyism (p. 200).
73 Cf. Dennis Cooke, *Persecuting Zeal: A Portrait of Ian Paisley*, Dingle, Kerry:
    Brandon Publishers, 1996, p. 79f. The governor and his wife were violently
    jostler, causing Lady Erskine to fall ill.
74 James McAuley, "The Emergence of New Loyalism," *Changing Shades of
    Orange and Green: Redefining the Union and Nation in Contemporary Ireland*,
    John Coakley (ed.), Dublin: University College Press, 2002, pp 114, 117.
75 Fran Brearton, *The Great War in Irish Poetry: W. B. Yeats to Michael Longley*,
    Oxford: Oxford University Press, 2000, p. 157.
76 Akenson, op. cit., p. 293.
77 John Coakley, "Conclusion: New Strains of Unionism and Nationalism,"
    Coakley, op. cit., p. 138.
78 Ibid., p. 1.
79 Cited in Steve Bruce, *God Save Ulster: The Religion and Politics of Paisleyism*,
    Oxford: Clarendon Press, 1986, pp. 269–270.

V

The Crucified Nation
PALESTINE

In modern Palestinian nationalism, the poet, especially the poet in exile, once again becomes the natural scribe of national sentiment, pouring his (sometimes her) soul into sorrowful and impassioned laments for the murdered nation:

> They spread the glad tidings
> When they joined Him at the Last Supper,
> And before He walked,
> Dragging His cross along the path of thorns and rocks,
> They surrounded Him,
> Giving Him their vows,
> But, their eyelids heavy, they slept,
> Leaving Him behind.
> He grieved all alone,
> And reluctantly drank from the cup he shunned.
> He felt the chill of death in His blood,
> And sorrow's bitter taste in his mouth.
> Before dawn
> One betrayed Him,
> One denied Him,
> And the others fled.[1]

In subsequent verses, Jesus metamorphoses into Abel, another murder victim, and then into "virtuous" Job with his festering wounds; all, however, personify Palestine, the suffering and crucified object of the poet's adoration. Despite his choice of Christian symbolism, the author of these lines, 'Abd-al-Karim al-Sab'awi (1938–), is a Muslim, which seems surprising but which is explained by the degree to which Christian themes and images have permeated Palestinian culture and affected the popular discourse of the literary classes, whether Christian or Muslim.[2] The fact that Jerusalem, the political heart of the Palestinian collective identity, contains sacred sites dear to both religious communities has assisted a certain blending of Christian and Muslim motifs. Another Arab poet, in this case a communist member of the Israeli parliament (*Knesset*) as well as a former mayor of Nazareth (1977), Tawfiq Zayyad 1932–), also – in spite of dialectical materialism – readily employs Christian imagery in his romantic dream of national resurrection, significantly entitled *The Crucified One*:

My loved ones . . .
With flowers and sweets,
With all my love, I wait . . .
I, the earth, the moon,
The spring, the olives and the flowers wait . . .
Our thirsty groves await you,
Our alley and our vineyard,
And a thousand green verses
That can make the hard stones sprout leaves.

With flowers and sweets,
With all my love, I wait . . .
Watching for the wind
Blowing from the East,
Perchance it may bring us news
On its wings.
And perhaps one day, the river will cry,
"Arise and breathe again, crucified one,
Your long-gone people have returned."[3]

Other examples abound, for poetry, especially lyrical poetry, has long adorned the Arab genius, constituting a special and eloquent voice in Arabic culture.[4] Again and again Palestine is portrayed in figurative terms as a nation on the cross, cruelly slain yet mysteriously regenerative in death, the inspiration of all who contemplate its fate and drink from its bitter chalice. The poet Mu'in Bsisu (1930–), incidentally also a communist, could hardly be more explicit.

Cast your lots, people,
Who'll get my robe
after crucifixion?

The vinegar cup in my right hand,
the thorn crown on my head,
and the murderer has walked away free
while your son has been led
   To the cross.
But I shall not run
from the vinegar cup,
nor the crown of thorns.
I'll carve the nails of my cross from my own bones
and continue,
spilling drops of my blood onto this earth
For if I should not rip apart
   How would you be born from my heart?
   How would I be born from my heart?
   Oh, my people![5]

Golgotha, according to still another poet Jabra Ibrahim Jabra (1920–), was re-enacted in the Palestinian village of Dayr Yasin, the site of a savage massacre of local residents by Irgun and Stern Gang terrorists in 1948 when Jews and Arabs were at war. The bodies of the Arab victims, "young maidens and bleeding pregnant women," cast into a well by their assassins, inspired the Christian author to examine their fate in light of a more famous murder: "was Jesus crucified there once more?"[6] This particular slaughter of innocents soon assumed the proportions of a cosmic crime in Arab eyes, remaining to this day a festering sore on the Palestinian psyche.[7] From the mouth of the well, Jabra avers, from this "second Golgotha" will flow the "black lava" of retribution, presumably the vengeance of God.

Nineteen forty-eight was no ordinary year. In the trenchant phrase of yet another major Palestinian poet Mahmud Darwish (1942–), like B'sisu and Zayyad a communist, it was the "Palestinian year without end."[8] Perhaps more than his rivals, Darwish approximates in Palestinian nationalism the stature of Adam Mickiewicz in Polish nationalism as the supreme bard of national identity and tragic exile. He is also the author of the later Palestinian Declaration of Independence read from the *al-Aqsa* Mosque in November 1989 under an Israeli curfew.[9] The years 1948–49 was the time of the great catastrophe, the disaster known in Palestinian historiography as *al-Nakba*, when between 500,000 and 1,000,000 Palestinians became refugees, driven from their homes in either a deliberate expulsion or as a consequence of simple panic and fear. Controversy still rages around the true reasons for their flight and the issue of responsibility.[10] Whatever the real cause or causes of the sudden Arab departure, *al-Nakba*, like all defining events in history, has acquired mythic contours, and in historical myths exactly what happened and why it happened is largely beside the point; not facts *per se* but the manner in which facts are perceived and interpreted is what matters. The mass exodus, declares Mahmoud Abbas, the moderate current leader (president) of the Palestinian Authority, will remain forever etched on the Palestinian memory as a black and criminal day never to be forgotten.[11] Truly, the great catastrophe, together with such village catastrophes as Dayr Yasin, involved the cosmos itself, since it mirrored on an epic scale the classic human drama of good and evil, with evil ascendant. A paradisal Palestine, a veritable "land of musk and amber,"[12] a land of "peony and narcissus," a land of olive and almond trees and orange groves,[13] was despoiled and ravaged and transformed into a wasteland, with its children cast into oblivion. Since the latter, according to Darwish and other Palestinian annotators, were attached to the soil of their country in a mystical and even a biological fashion, their expulsion was truly a crime nonpareil. Lover was torn from lover in the most heartless of violations.

> This is the wedding without an end,
> In a boundless courtyard,
> On an endless night.
> This is the Palestinian wedding:
> Never will lover reach lover
> Except as martyr or fugitive.[14]

In a similar vein, Jabra also draws a contrast between the green and verdant country that once was and the frost and dust of the desert that now is, remembering the former nostalgically as the New Testament setting where angels once visited shepherds with songs of peace on earth and good will among human beings: the nativity of Christ.[15] Not only the people but the land itself, the poet implies, was crucified.

The crucifiers, who of course were Jewish, or to be more precise Zionist Jews, were and are regarded as alien Europeans who, because of their own rootless existence, utterly failed to understand the profound attachment to the Palestinian earth, its stones and orchards and blossoms, so intensely felt by the indigenous Palestinians. Olive trees in particular seem to have become sacred vessels in Palestinian literature of this sacramental union. Therefore, with some Arab complicity (the wealthy landowners who sold their estates and evicted their tenant farmers), the Zionists assaulted both the people and the land, razing Palestinian villages and crushing "the flowers on the hills," creating not only fugitives and martyrs but also thorny deserts with "valleys writhing in hunger."[16] Although the Zionist intruders imported Western technology, changing the face of Palestine with their trucks and automobiles and "hybrid green and blue signs," the land nevertheless remained unequivocally Arab to the Arab lyricists, singing with "Arab affection" to the Arab soul.[17] Zionist rootlessness and Palestinian rootedness, Zionist superficiality and Palestinian depth, Zionist *Gesellschaft* and Palestinian *Gemeinschaft*:* these contrasts inform the Palestinian writers of both poetry and prose. To remove the Palestinians from hearth and home – the geographical space that constitutes their *alter ego* – is to damage their inner spiritual being, causing all so uprooted to languish in the metaphorical desert of the world, dreaming of paradise lost, their vanished Eden. "Oh Palestine!" cries the poet Abu Salmas, "Nothing more beautiful, more precious, more pure!"[18] "Lost paradise!" cries the poet Mahmud al-Hut, " . . . Torn asunder your people, Wandering under every star."[19]

Paradise lost: a cosmic theme if there ever was one, and surely as powerful a literary and political motif as can be found in the vast corpus of irredentist literature in the many languages of the world. Paradise, of course, the land of Palestine was not, whether under British or Ottoman rule or in earlier centuries, but the romantic mind always endows the past, especially the *ante bellum* past, with the utopian virtues of a golden age. The greater the misery of the present, the more splendid the vanished glory of former times and the more poignant the dream of return. When this dream is intermingled with religious components in a theologically constructed universe, its cosmic dimensions loom large: God, the biblical God of Jewish, Christian and Muslim monotheism, is a God of justice and all wrongs must be set right. If the cosmic order ordained by God has been shattered by a monumental human crime, as *al-Nakba* certainly seems to the displaced and violated Palestinians, the cosmic order must be restored – paradise must be regained – so that the universe can recover its moral equilibrium. In this manner, Palestinian nationalism, whether Christian or Muslim or communist, is invested with transcendence, causing the struggle with Jewish nationalism (the state of Israel) to assume a white and black character: a Manichaean dualism As their situation worsened, especially in the refugee camps spawned by their forced exodus, the exiles consoled themselves by dwelling on the righteousness of their cause and the loveliness of their former abode: the perfect garden that once was Palestine. In such terms the eminent Palestinian intellectual Sari Nusseibeh speaks of his mother's lost orange groves – the

---

* Contractual society versus community.

"sweetest on earth" – in an idyllic and "magical dreamland."[20] How agonizing was the contrast between its lost ineffable delights and the dismal nature of exilic existence!

While many Palestinians remained within the borders of the Jewish state, suddenly aliens in a radically transformed milieu, many others fled to Gaza and the West Bank, where they later came under Israeli military rule (1967), and others to the surrounding Arab countries, Lebanon, Syria and Jordan, where their welcome was less than warm. Exile, however, is a psychological as well as a physical state of being, and the trauma of 1948–49 affected all Palestinians, those left behind as well as those scattered abroad. Thus Palestinian nationalism, at first only a local variant of pan-Arabism, developed a separate identity, distinguishing the Palestinian nation from the 'Arab nation,' that is to say, the Arab world as such. The fact that many of the refugees were rural in origin served to nurture this sense of distinctiveness; wrenched from their farms and villages, families which cherished the close communion between the tiller and the soil grew passionate in their nostalgia.[21] Patriotism in its classical sense, the love of the *patria*, the love of one's native hearth and home, flourished in the camps, along with many less exalted feelings, namely resentment, alienation, despair, anger and zealotry, the final fruit of which was terrorism. Because of these dispiriting frames of mind, patriotism readily turned into nationalism, producing a new generation of nationalist movements dedicated to refuting the famous judgment once pronounced by Prime Minister Golda Meir of Israel that there were no Palestinians.[22] Her words only served to inflame the feelings of the dispossessed. To the Palestinians themselves, Palestine was always a nation but a nation asleep prior to the 1948–49 war; history and the Zionists rudely awakened it. If it did not 'exist' before 1948, it certainly did exist in Arab minds after the Arab defeat, although its existence, unlike the existence of the new proclaimed Jewish state, took the form of an unrealized ideal: a nation in search of a state. In this sense, it was not dissimilar to the submerged Poland of the nineteenth century, although Poland unlike Palestine had formerly been a nation-state.

If Palestinian nationalism was bred and nourished by adversity, so was its arch antagonist Jewish nationalism, another modern movement with romantic as well as religious affinities. If the Palestinians thought (and still think) longingly of their idealized homeland in their refugee havens, so did the early Zionists in their east European Jewish enclaves, seeking to alleviate the pogroms of the nineteenth and twentieth centuries with dreams of Zion, the revered land of their biblical ancestors. Clear parallels can be traced between the two exiles, the camp and the ghetto, despite the caesura in time, for "alienation, homelessness and a sense of the unreality of the world"[23] was as much a property of Jewish experience as of Palestinian experience. It is of the utmost importance to remember that Israel, as one Jewish philosopher has declared, was fashioned by people with deeply bruised psyches."[24] Judaism itself as a biblical religion is indissolubly wedded to the Israel of the Hebrew Scriptures (the Old Testament), even if the exact nature of the relationship between the people and the land is subject to different theological interpretations. Exile and return have always been powerful elements in Jewish thought, whether rabbinical, mystical or secular, and nothing has ever diminished this fundamental paradigm. Zionism itself was thoroughly modern in its intellectual cradle, but even the secular Zionists who did not believe in God nevertheless believed in their tangible religiously inspired Jewish birthright, the Promised Land. As with the later Palestinians, the greater the anguish and hence the injustice of the present, the more urgent and necessary its amelioration, something that could only be accomplished by returning to the one place on earth that seemed to offer genuine respite for Jewish bodies and Jewish souls, *Eretz Israel*. So, for example, declared the early Russian Zionist Moshe Lieb Lilienblum (1843–1910);[25] he was not alone in thinking of the Jewish fatherland in semi-utopian terms.

The Zionist enterprise cannot be reduced to a simple reflex action against antisemitism, but the long Jewish vale of tears, often styled the lachrymose view of Jewish history, certainly had more than a little to do with its emergence in the nineteenth and twentieth centuries. For Israel, meaning the Jewish people rather than the Jewish nation-state, is also a crucified nation, indeed, because of the European holocaust (or *Shoah*), a nation on the cross in a far more literal and graphic sense than most other victimized human collectivities, although genocide and its cousin ethnic cleansing represent a sinister and rising phenomenon in our age.* Purim, the biblical tale of Esther who saved her people from mass slaughter in ancient Persia, has become a master narrative of the razor's edge on which Jews so often have been forced to tread, whether or not the biblical account is factually true (it almost certainly is not[26]). Like Palestinian poets, occasional Jewish poets such as Emma Lazarus of Statue of Liberty fame have also invoked Christian imagery in order to depict Jewish suffering:

Where is the Hebrew fatherland?
The folk of Christ is sore betrayed;

---

* I omit the tortured debate as to whether the holocaust was unique among the genocides of the modern period.

The Son of Man is bruised and banned,
Nor finds whereon to lay his head.
His cup is gall, his meat is tears,
His Passion lasts a thousand years.[27]

That the State of Israel is sometimes known as the 'holocaust state' is hardly surprising, although in fact somewhat misleading since its basic structural foundations existed before 1945 and since many serious tensions arose between holocaust survivors after their flight from Europe and indigenous Jews, amounting at times to a "strange wall" of misunderstanding and discord.[28] Nonetheless the dark apprehension of another holocaust became a constant feature of post-war Jewish life in Israel as well as the Diaspora, casting its shadow over the politics of the Middle East. This omnipresent fear, which every terrorist act serves to intensify, has greatly compounded the tragedy of the region, for Jews as well as Palestinians are tempted to place their conflict in a cosmic setting, each seeing the other as despoiler and crucifier. Is not death – the massacre of Jews in Hebron (1929), the massacre of Arabs in Dayr Yasin and Kafr Qasim (1956), the massacre of Israeli Olympic athletes in Munich (1972), the massacre of Arabs in Hebron by a deranged physician (1994), the seemingly endless cycle of murder and counter-murder – the choreographer of this passion play?

While the Palestinian *via dolorosa* is not as old as the Jewish *via dolorosa* (unless one traces its origins to the mediaeval crusades), it did not begin in 1948. The mass flight known in Palestinian historiography as *al-Nakba* was anticipated by an earlier flight of about 40,000 Palestinians to adjacent Arab countries following the suppression of the Great Arab Revolt (1936–1939) by British arms. This revolt, prompted by a number of causes, including labour struggles pitting Jews against Arabs and local anger at mounting Jewish land acquisitions, burst into flames with the death of the anti-British and anti-Zionist insurgent 'Iz-al-Din al-Qassam, who fell in a battle with the British police in 1935. A religious figure whose mindset was Islamic to the core and who liked to deliver his sermons with a gun or sword in his hands,[29] al-Qassam almost immediately assumed the status of a martyr among his followers, bestowing on the Palestinian cause a holy aura. Because of the populist character of the revolt – peasants and the urban poor joined the insurrection – the national idea captivated the masses as well as the elite, the *fellahin* as well as the *effendi*, instilling a powerful sense of Palestinian nationhood a decade prior to the birth of the Jewish state. This folk nationalism, with its European romantic affinities (except, of course, the Muslim factor, but

'Palestinianism' rather than Islam or Christianity became the index of the new national consciousness[30]) bequeathed its fiery spirit to the militant Palestinian rebel groups of later times, especially those with an appetite for martyrdom.[31] Once the Palestinian nation was conceived, moreover, the mythical and ideological fabrications that attend all nationalisms made their expected appearance. As a consequence, the modern Palestinians suddenly became the descendants of the ancient Canaanites and Edomites who were overrun in biblical times by the Hebrew invaders. As "Arab Canaanites," their claim to the land instantly acquired a greater validity than the rival Zionist claim, also based on antiquity.[32] History, however, as James Parkes pointed out long ago, supports neither side: the shifting sands of population change as empire succeeded empire and culture succeeded culture render all historical arguments relative and all land claims futile.[33]

If the latter-day Canaanites and Edomites discovered themselves by fighting the latter-day crusaders in British and Zionist guise, it does not follow that Palestinian nationalism was only a reaction against British rule and Jewish immigration. Nationalism was already afoot in the Middle East, a legacy of Arab resistance to the Ottoman Empire during the First World War as well as subsequent Western (British and French) imperial intrusions. Even in Ottoman times the word 'Palestine' (*Filastin*) was employed in the Arab press, and in 1914 the more significant term 'Palestinian nation' (*al-umma al-filastiniyya*) made its debut.[34] Traumatic events such as the French expulsion of King Faisal from Damascus in 1920 in order to seize his kingdom for themselves – a fruit of the Sykes–Picot agreement between Britain and France (1916) – greatly inflamed the Arab world, stirring a major "Arab awakening" as well as a pan-Arab nationalism in which language once again was seen as the essence of the nation.[35] This romantic concept, plainly derived from Herder, was promoted by certain Arab intellectuals of the day who fell in love with German rather than British or French ideas.[36] Arabic signified Arabness, turning the Arab countries into a single vast nation, a grand if not grandiose conception strongly promoted by the Egyptian strongman Gamal Abdel Nasser (Nasir), its arch-apostle. The transcendent vision of universal Arab nationhood still permeates contemporary Arab thought, although pan-Arabism as a political force disintegrated after the collapse of the United Arab Republic of Egypt and Syria (1961) and after the Six-Day War with Israel (1967), a débâcle described by one authority as the Arab Waterloo.[37] Palestinianism, or the incipient distinction between Palestinian Arabs and other Arabs, had its theoretical origins around 1918 but its apogee after 1948, when the national consciousness steadily deepened.[38] As we have seen, Palestinian suffering – the crucified nation – became its leitmotif.

The crucified Palestinian nation, sometimes personified as a beautiful woman, is not a creature of poetry alone; she appears also in visual art, for example, the spectacular large painting entitled 'The Conquered Land."[39] Suffering, however, as in other religiously infused nationalisms, represents more than simple victimization; it contains the seeds of resurrection, the manifestation of a new creation, a higher and better Palestinian, the resistance hero who will slay his crucifiers. This new Palestinian born of revolution thus becomes the "quasi-religious icon" of the great struggle to liberate his country from Zionist oppression.[40] His counterpart in Jewish nationalism is the *sabra*, the defiant Israel-born new Jew of the new age unafraid to fight and perish rather than submit to his enemies, as did the meek and passive 'holocaust Jew' who, according to popular belief, walked like a lamb to his slaughter.[41] Masada, the alleged site of a collective suicide during the Roman/Judean War (73), was adopted by the early Zionists as a symbol of Jewish heroism: "Never again shall Masada fall!' Unfortunately, like so many national myths, Masada was also a fabrication, since the Sicarii who dwelt in the ancient fortress were far from heroic, having specialized in the assassination of other Jews. Nor is it certain that they died in the splendid manner that Israeli civil religion claims.[42] The new Palestinian in mortal combat with the new Jew, each, like the Germanic Siegfried, the product of the new age, each the child of oppression, each in search of political redemption, comprises the blind and tragic clash of two nationalisms over the same land. In the Palestinian case, a powerful dichotomy between the poles of sacrificial suffering and glorious resistance, immortalized by the martyred poet 'Abd al-Rahim Mahmud (1913–1948), remains the basic paradigm of national defiance, the supreme Palestinian narrative.[43]

> The slain motherland called for our struggle
> and my heart leapt with joy.
> I raced the winds, but did not boast.
> Isn't it my simple duty to redeem my country?
> I carried my soul in my hands asking
> any who feared death: do you hesitate
> before the enemy?
> Would you sit still when your country begs for your
> help?
> Would you back away from facing the enemy? . . .
> The motherland needs mighty defenders

who meet aggression
but never complain,
true lions on the battlefield.

People of my country, our days of sacrifice have
arrived;
they shine, radiant, across the hills of this holy
land.
Redeemed by our young men too proud
to endure oppression,
what can we do but fight bravely
when the fire's kindled?
March on, to the field! Pour fire
on the heads of the enemy everywhere....

Don't give up even if the world should face you
with weapons from every direction
unite, unite everywhere!
If Palestine should be lost while you still live,
I'll say: our people have
abandoned the path.[44]

Hence emerged the cult of the warrior-martyr, and along with it the
female image of the mother of the martyr, another icon in Palestinian
nationalism. Not only is the nation conceived as a beautiful woman but
also as a woman in excruciating pain. What could be more emblematic
of the national plight?[45]

The day Yasser was shot his mother turned
to stone; draped with the flag, his makeshift shroud,
she held her ground at the deserted town
square. Each chilly dawn she clutched a torch
of modest flowers – jasmine, daisies, and roses
from her garden – while bewildered soldiers
driving by, returning from their night shift, wondered
at the mist-clad apparition vaguely
reminiscent of a statue somewhere.[46]

As in Irish nationalism (one recalls the Manchester martyrs), funeral
processions for the martyred Palestinian dead have turned into regular
occasions for nationalistic effusion, both cries of solidarity with the latest

sacrificial victim and paeans to the infinite glory of martyrdom itself. "In the spirit and in the blood we sacrifice our life for you, oh martyr."[47] A religious halo encircles the head of the political martyr, once again fusing Christian and Muslim themes and symbols. Islam, in its Shi'ite form, has long contained a religiously sanctioned sacrificial strain because of the peculiar deaths of 'Ali, the prophet's son-in-law, in 661, and the latter's son Husain in 680. Since, however, the great majority of Palestinian Muslims belong to the Sunni rather than the Shi'ite branch of Islam, it is doubtful if this tradition has played more than a minor role in Gaza and the West Bank. Instead, the image of the holy warrior (*mujahid*) seems to inform their poetic declamations. Nevertheless the motif of the righteous man wrongly slain seeks to have embedded itself in Muslim as well as Christian thought.

The ongoing dialectic of suffering and resistance with its necessary synthesis in the celebration of martyrdom found its most glorious hour during the *Intifada* or popular uprising in the Gaza Strip and West Bank that began in 1987. In this highly publicized conflict, the Palestinian 'David,' meaning the Arab youths who cast stones at Israeli tanks, fought the Israeli 'Goliath,' thereby managing to invert the ancient biblical paradigm. (Israel, on the other hand, usually sees itself as a David *redivivus* in mortal combat with the Goliath of a hostile and often antisemitic modern world.) The "children of the stone" with their shrouded faces soon turned into new iconic figures to be extolled in verse and legend.[48]

Hail the stone!
Hail the stone!
Hail the stone![49]

Elemental and of the earth, therefore actual fragments of the beloved land, the very stones themselves, flung by the weak against the strong, were elevated into marks of defiance, causing the "glass house" of Israel to be shattered.[50] If death ensued, death ensued, but, as in all nationalisms, the "pure and immaculate" blood of the murdered hero or heroine only serves to fertilize the sacred soil of the nation.[51] The old holy martyr al-Qassam indubitably kindled the flames of Palestinianism when he fell in battle. Did not Jeanne d'Arc, Robert Emmet, Wolfe Tone and Patrick Pearse also accomplish in death what they could not accomplish in life?

The *Intifada* did not succeed and could not have succeeded in ending the Israeli occupation of the conquered territories, despite a wave of international sympathy for the battered Palestinians (a great propaganda victory). However, it did succeed in exposing once again the impotence as well as the arrogance of power, that is to say, the notion, always popular in bellicose circles, that sheer force is the best way to solve disagreeable problems and that if a small amount of force fails to achieve the desired result, more force should be employed. Following the heady intoxication of victory in the Six-Day War and its sudden ascendancy on the battlefield, the Jewish state, as the Israeli novelist Amos Oz has written, intermingled religious and political ecstasy with the "rituals of militarism and the cult of generals."[52] It was at this historical moment that David metamorphosed into Goliath, and Goliath (the combined Arab nations and their armies) into David. The irony has a bitter taste. Strength, moreover, as in the case of the biblical Goliath, is never without its Achilles' heel, and thus vulnerable in one way or another to those who dare to stand against it. No only young men but also women, children and the elderly, the weakest of the weak, picked up stones in the course of the uprising, stirring Palestinian pride to the utmost degree.[53] It was during the *Intifada* that the proud new Palestinian, the revolutionary analogue of the proud new Jew, was fully and finally cast in a heroic mould.[54] The spectacle of children battling uniformed men armed to the teeth created an intolerable situation for the Israeli military, as the stone-throwers probably realized. A long-standing symbol of "unity, strength and morality" in the Jewish state, the army was ill-equipped to deal with this unprecedented mode of resistance and many of its soldiers suffered acute personal distress.[55]

If the *Intifada* gave birth to a new type of Palestinian, it also gave birth to a new phase in the quest for Palestinian independence. In the war of leaflets that accompanied the insurgency, a fault line appeared between nationalists who wished to recover the entire land of Palestine (as traditionally defined) and nationalists who were willing to settle for a Palestinian state adjacent to the Jewish state. *Dar-al Islam*, the doctrine that Palestinian soil was also Muslim soil – was not Palestine the sacred land of Muhammed's heavenly ascension? – required the abolition of Israel and the establishment of Islamic rule over the entire region. In this spirit, *Hamas*,★ an offspring of the older Muslim Brotherhood, sought and still seeks to raise the "banner of Allah over every grain of soil."[56] By way of contrast, the Palestine Liberation Organization (PLO) and its various factions appealed to Israeli as well as Arab support for the establishment of a Palestinian state in the occupied territories, albeit with Arab Jerusalem as its capital.[57] No less devoted to the blood of the martyrs than *Hamas*, they still envisaged the reins of power in both Muslim and Christian hands rather than Muslim hands alone. Should that day ever

---

★ An acronym signifying Islamic Resistance Movement. It also means "zeal".

arrive, the towers of the churches as well as the minarets of the mosques will be decorated with Palestinian flags in a glorious display of national solidarity. The "Zionist machine of occupation" will be crushed and the "usurping Zionists" pushed back from the realms wrongly seized by their forces.[58] Pragmatism rather than fanaticism typified most of their demands, even when the souls of the slain patriots that "hover in the skies" – one is reminded of Maude Gonne's dancing spirits of the slain Irish – over the crucified homeland joined the fray, promising laurel wreaths of victory to the children of the revolution.[59] Nationalism after all is nationalism, and cannot be gainsaid.

Nationalist or not, the late Palestinian chieftain Yasir Arafat, whose characteristic headdress was in itself a token of national identity,★ acted as a pragmatist or perhaps one could say a realist when he decided to recognize the state of Israel in 1988 on the basis of the United Nations resolutions of 1967 calling for Israeli withdrawal from its recent conquests. Tacitly, therefore, as far as the Palestinian leadership was concerned, the dream of a larger Palestine was abandoned in favour of a more modest nation-state comprised of Gaza and the West Bank. The emergence in 1992 of a less intransigent government in Israel under Yitzhak Rabin enabled negotiations (at first secret) between Israelis and Palestinians in Oslo, Norway, the fruit of which was an accord in 1993 of unprecedented promise. Mutual recognition *pro tempore*, the renunciation of terrorist tactics on Arafat's part, Israeli withdrawal from the occupied territories beginning with Gaza and Jericho, the election of an interim Palestinian civil authority (council) as a prelude to a final resolution of all outstanding issues in five years (1998), were its major provisions. Was freedom and peace at last on the horizon, was a new 'Spring of Nations' imminent? The flowering of hope, alas, proved ephemeral as a result of the many cross purposes and tensions concealed beneath the surface of the agreement, dooming it virtually from the day it was signed. In particular, the emotionally charged question of the Jewish settlements outside the bounds of the Jewish state loomed as an insurmountable barrier in the path of future progress, along with the bitter struggle over Jerusalem. Neither nationalism, Jewish or Palestinian, would or could surrender its inner romantic essence without violent repercussions; violence, in fact, was predestined after Oslo, and violence soon came.

The settlements, which, at least as far as official rhetoric was

---

★ The *kufia* or headscarf was adopted by early guerilla fighters, becoming in time a national symbol.

102

concerned, were established initially for reasons of security – a protective string of small Jewish outposts – acquired a more ideological rationale after the *Likud*-led regime of Menachem Begin came to power in 1977 with its vision of a greater Israel. Hence the fiercely nationalistic *Gush Emunim* (Bloc of the Faithful) movement, founded after the 1973 war, was allowed to sponsor scores of new settlers in short order, with many ramifications for Jewish–Arab relations and the future of the entire region. Not classical Zionism, except perhaps the school of thought associated with the revisionist Vladimir Jabotinsky,[60] but a religiously infused (messianic) territorialism now triumphed over earlier less promethean forms of Jewish nationalism, causing Arabic names and Palestinian land claims to be eradicated in "Judea" and "Samaria" as if many centuries had not intervened between the ancient kingdom and the modern nation-state. Despite much uneasiness in Israel regarding this rapid expansionism, despite the pangs of conscience suffered by some members of the Israeli Defense Forces (as in the 'Peace Now' movement), settlement momentum grew, abetted by successive Israeli prime ministers even after the Oslo accord. Since what is done cannot easily be undone, and since only the breadth of a hair separates *de facto* from *de jure*, it became obvious that the terms of eventual peace could only become less and less palatable as time passed. Predictably, therefore, the Palestinians erupted, striking at the settlements with mounting fury. Other frustrations – travel restrictions, work restrictions, passport restrictions, economic deprivation, the heavy hand of military occupation – added their wormwood to the Palestinian cup of woe. Whereas guerilla warfare had old antecedents, the infamous suicide bomber was essentially a creature of the post-Oslo era and its assorted disappointments. A new species of martyrdom, this peculiar form of mass murder sanctified by religious and political nihilism seized the stage centre during the second (*al-Aqsa*) *Intifada* in 2000.

The new uprising began when Ariel Sharon, later prime minister of Israel, protected by an armed escort, chose to visit the Temple Mount, the site of both the Dome of the Rock and the *al-Aqsa* mosque, at a sensitive and dangerous moment following the Camp David fiasco in July 2000, delivering a lethal blow to any chances of Israeli-Palestinian accord.[61] His act (September 28) was symbolic: an assertion of Jewish sovereignty on the part of a known patron of the *Gush Emunim* zealots and their messianic nationalism. *Al-Aqsa*, the third most holy shrine in Islam, the place from which the prophet was believed to have ascended to heaven, had been violated several times in the past by anti-Muslim agitators. Set on fire in 1969 and almost blown up in 1984, the mosque had long inspired poetic ardour, sometimes in the form of grim elegies about the Palestinian future, as in a lament composed by 'Abd al-Rahim Mahmud on the occasion of a much earlier visit (1935) by the Saudi prince Sa'ud ibn 'Abd al-'Aziz:

> The Aqsa Mosque, oh Prince, have you come to pay reverence to it,
>> or to bid it farewell before it is lost,
> a sanctuary to be ravaged by every mutilated runaway slave,
>> by every roving vagabond?
> And tomorrow, how near it is! For us nothing will remain
>> but remorse and flowing tears.[62]

In the mind of the poet, turning to a familiar and frequent Arab conceit, the original Zionists were latter-day crusaders, "wild beasts from the West" intent on devouring Palestine and her children, not to mention the Muslim faith itself, as had their European ancestors.[63] Not surprisingly, the intrusion of Ariel Sharon on Muslim sacred soil sixty-five years later was interpreted in the same sinister light, as was the Anglo-American invasion of Iraq in 2003.

Sharon, however, a man with a ruthless reputation, astonished the world by forcibly evicting Jewish settlers from Gaza in 2005, thereby incurring the fury of the Israeli political and religious irredentists, although a debate still rages with respect to his true motives. Had the lifelong *sabra* experienced a genuine change of heart or was he merely engaged in an elaborate game of power politics, deflecting international attention from the new 'Berlin wall' under construction and a score of further encroachments in the Left Bank? His precipitous departure from the *Likud* party in order to form a new political entity (*Kadima*) lends itself to either view, although the prime minister's earlier actions and his old call for Arab "Bantustans" cast suspicion on his intentions.[64] Since, however, a massive stroke struck him down scarcely a month later, leaving him alive but incapacitated, the 'Palestinian problem' and its solution has fallen into other hands. In the meantime, the torments of the region persist, greatly aggravated by the victory of an unrepentant *Hamas*, more than ever obsessed with the destruction of the Jewish state, in the Palestinian legislative elections of 2006. A state of virtual Palestinian civil war, reflecting the civil conflicts in other Arab societies – Lebanon, Iraq – and the general disorder of the Middle East, has now descended on the beloved land of the nationalist poets, the land of musk and amber. When the interests, fears and passions of external powers – Arab and non-Arab, Muslim and non-Muslim, Western and non-Western – are added to the volatile brew, no one should be surprised that the crucified nation still finds itself on the cross, forced indefinitely to await its third day.

Notes

1 'Abd-al-Karim al-Sab'awi, "Three Poems to Palestine," cited in *The Palestinian Wedding: A Bilingual Anthology of Contemporary Palestinian Resistance Poetry*, trans. A. M. Elmessiri, Washington, D.C.: Three Continents Press, 1982, p. 165.

2 Ibid., p. 18.

3 Tawfiq Zayyad, "The crucified one," ibid. (cited), p. 177.

4 A. M. Elmessiri, "The Palestinian Wedding: Major Themes of Contemporary Palestinian Resistance Poetry," *Journal of Palestine Studies* (Vol. 10/no. 3/ Spring 1981), p. 79.

5 Mu'in Bsisu, "The Vinegar Cup," (trans.), cited in *Anthology of Modern Palestinian Literature*, Salma Khadra Jayyusi (editor), New York: Columbia University Press, 1992, p. 135.

6 Jabra Ibrahim Jabra, "The mouth of the well," Elmessiri, op. cit., p. 47.

7 Baruch Kimmerling & Joel S. Migdal, *Palestinians: The Making of a People*, New York: The Free Press, 1993, p. 152.

8 Mahmud Darwish, "Blessed be that which has not come!," Elmessiri, op. cit., p. 203.

9 See Sari Nusseibeth, *Once Upon a Country: A Palestinian Life*, New York: Farrar, Straus & Giroux, 2007, pp. 296–297.

10 Cf. Benny Morris, "The Origins of the Palestinian Refugee Problem," *New Perspectives on Israeli History: The Early Years of the State*, Laurence J.. Silberstein (ed.), New York: New York University Press, 1991, p. 42f. As far as responsibility for the flight is concerned, it seems to rest with both the Arab and Jewish leadership of the day.

11 (Toronto) *Globe and Mail*, May 16, 2005.

12 Abu Salmas, "I Love You More," (trans.), Jayyusi, op. cit., p. 97.

13 Jabra, "In the Deserts of Exile," (trans.), Elmessiri, op. cit., pp. 69–70.

14 Darwish, "Blessed be that which has not come!," (trans.) Ibid., p. 197.

15 Jabra, "In the deserts of exile," ibid., pp. 69–70.

16 Ibid.

17 Laila 'Alush, "The path of affection," ibid., pp. 173–17.

18 Abu Salmas, "I Love You More."

19 Cited in Barbara McKean Parmenter, *Giving Voice to Stones: Place and Identity in Palestinian Literature*, Austin: University of Texas Press, 1994, p. 47.

20 Nusseibeh, *Once Upon a Country: A Palestinian Life*, New York: Farrar, Straus & Giroux, 2007, p. 67.

21 Yezid Sayigh, *Armed Struggle and the Search for State: The Palestinian National Movement 1949–1993*, Oxford: Clarendon Press, 1997, p. 46.

22 See Rashid Khalidi, *Palestinian Identity: The Construction of Modern National Consciousness*, New York: Columbia University Press, 1997, pp. 179–181.

Her comments appeared originally in *The Sunday Times* (June 15, 1969). Golda Meir clearly intended to undermine Palestinian geopolitical claims. As Arabs like other Arabs, they possessed no distinctive local identity in her eyes and consequently no reason not to live elsewhere than on Palestinian soil.

23 Parmenter, op. cit., p. 68.

24 David Har(t)man?, cited in Nusseibeh, op. cit., p. 485.

25 "Let us pay no heed to the renegades trying to lead us away from our father-land . . . This is the land in which our fathers have found rest since time immemorial . . . Let us go now to the only land in which we will find respite for our souls that have been harried by murderers for these thousands of years." Moshe Lieb Lilienblum, "The Way of Return," cited in *The Zionist Idea: A Historical Analysis and Reader*, Arthur Hertzberg (ed.), New York: Harper & Row, 1959, pp. 172–173.

26 See Neil Caplan, "Psychological Obstacles to Israeli Reconciliation with the Palestinians," *Israeli and Palestinian Identities in History and Literature*, Kamal Abdel-Malek & David C. Jacobson (eds), New York: St. Martin's Press, 1991, pp. 65–68.

27 Emma Lazarus, cited in Matthew Hoffman, *From Rebel to Rabbi: Reclaiming Jesus and the Making of Modern Jewish Culture*, Stanford: Stanford University Press, 2007, p. 177.

28 Cf. Tom Segev, *The Seventh Million: The Israelis and the Holocaust*, trans. Haim Watzman, New York: Hill & Wang, 1993, p. 179.

29 Kimmerling & Migdal, op. cit., pp. 61–62.

30 Cf. Ted Swedenburg, *Memories of Revolt: The 1936–1939 Rebellion and the Palestinian National Past*, Minneapolis: University of Minnesota Press, 1995, p. 89f.

31 Cf. Helena Lindholm Schultz, *The Reconstruction of Palestinian Nationalism: Between Revolution and Statehood*, Manchester: Manchester University Press, 1999, p. 29.

32 Ibid., p. 80.

33 "In all the 3,500 years of its recorded history it (the land) has never been exclusively the house of a single people." James Parkes, *Whose Land? A History of the Peoples of Palestine*, Harmondsworth, Middlesex: Penguin Books, 1970, p. 311.

34 Cf. Rashid Khalidi, "The Formation of Palestinian Identity: The Critical Years 1917–1923," *Rethinking Nationalism in the Arab Middle East*, James Jankowski & Israel Gershoni (eds), New York: Columbia University Press, 1997, p. 176.

35 Ibid., p. 24.

36 Cf. Elie Chalala, "Arab Nationalism: A Bibliographic Essay," *Pan-Arabism and Arab Nationalism: The Continuing Debate*, Tawfic E. Farah (ed.), Boulder: Westview Press, 1987, pp. 36–37.

37 Fouad Ajami, "The End of Pan-Arabism," Farah, op. cit., p. 98.

38 Schultz, op. cit., p. 26.

39 Kimmerling & Migdal, op. cit., final illustration, pp. 204–205.

40 Ibid., p. 233.

41 As the Warsaw ghetto uprising (April 19–May 16, 1943) testifies, the holo-caust Jew did not always submit meekly to his fate.

42 See Nachman Ben-Yehuda, *The Masada Myth: Collective Memory and Mythmaking in Israel*, Madison: University of Wisconsin Press, 1995, passim.

43 Schultz, op. cit., p. 37.

44 'Abd al-Rahim Mahmud, "Call of the Motherland," Jayyusi, op. cit., pp. 210–211.

45 Schultz, op. cit., p. 41.

46 Hanan Mikha'il Ashrawi, "Metamorphosis," Jayyusi, op. cit., p. 335.

47 Cited in Schultz, op. cit., p. 65.

48 Kimmerling & Migdal, op. cit., p. 262.

49 Ibid. (cited), p. 263.

50 mi Elad-Bouskila, *Modern Palestinian Literature and Culture*, London: Frank Cass, 1999, p. 100 (cited).

51 Schultz, op. cit. (cited), p. 68.

52 Amos Oz, *In the Land of Israel*, New York: Random House, 1984, p. 132.

53 Elad-Bouskila, op. cit., p. 127.

54 Cf. Ruth Margolies Beiter, *The Path to Mass Rebellion: An Analysis of Two Intifadas*, Lanham, Maryland: Lexington Books, 2004, p. 99.

55 Ibid., p. 98.

56 Shaul Mishal & Reuben Aharoni, *Speaking Stones: Communiqués from the Intifada Underground*, Syracuse: Syracuse University Press, 1994, p. 30 (cited).

57 Ibid., pp. 140–145.

58 Ibid., p. 140.

59 Ibid., p. 141.

60 Hailed as the Garibaldi of the Zionist movement by his admirers and the Mussolini by his critics, Vladimir Jabotinsky (1880–1940) broke with Chaim Weizmann and the Zionist mainstream to found his own revisionist party. He favoured mass Jewish immigration and the transformation of Palestine into a Jewish state. The Arabs would not be expelled but would be required to accept minority status and its disabilities if they chose to live within its bounds. Of course, like other Zionists, Jabotinsky did not acknowledge the existence of a separate Palestinian Arab identity with its own national rights; Arabs were simply Arabs and could live equally well in the surrounding Arab countries. Some of his later followers (e.g. *Irgun Zvai Leumi*, the Stern Gang) engaged in terrorism.

61 The American sponsored attempt at Camp David to revolve the impasse between Israel, represented by the then prime minister Ehud Barak, and the Palestinian leadership represented by Yasir Arafat

62 'Abd al-Rahim Mahmud, "The Aqsa Mosque," Parmenter, op. cit. (cited), p. 38.

64 Nusseibeh, op. cit., p. 524.

Conclusion

"Historically, Western nationalism, patriotism, and religion have twisted around each other like sinuous vines."[1] This dictum is confirmed and illustrated by the five case studies – Poland, France, Germany, Ireland and Palestine – which comprise our text. Modern nationalism, despite its secular origins in the Enlightenment and in the romantic reaction to the dogmas of rationalism, contains a genuine religious component, as nationality is a matter of the spirit as well as of the flesh. In bestowing a sense of personal and communal identity as well as a sense of vocation on all who worship at its altar, the idea of the nation assumes a meaning and importance above and beyond the mundane concerns of daily life. Because of this trait, nationalism can and has been described on occasion as a secular pietism or even a secular religion, especially in the critical thought of the twentieth century.[2] Indeed, because of its destructive elements, it also can and has been described as a demonic religion, or that which is both holy and evil at the same time. Like the Molochs of the ancient world, the gods of modern nationalism as well as the gods of political revolution feed on sacrificial victims, devouring at times even their own children. This demonic potential is evident in the fury that nationalistic emotions have unleashed in the violent conflicts of our day. It is also evident in the facile appropriation of biblical and Christian symbols in nations with Christian cultures or cultures strongly influenced by Christianity: hence the 'Christ-nation' and the 'crucified nation' of our five arbitrarily selected nationalisms.

By assigning the holiness of Christ to particular peoples and countries, nationalist poets, novelists, preachers and politicians exalt the nation unduly and promote a self-righteousness that is both dangerous in itself and conducive to acts of moral blindness. To transpose religious categories onto national collectivities is to sink into dreams and delusions, as the countless wars past and present between 'elect' and 'chosen' nations, each convinced of its own special status, each convinced that heaven, Jewish, Christian or Muslim,★ (footnote overleaf) is on its side, serves as

ample proof. Yet in one form or another all authentic nationalisms seem
to fall into this temptation, great powers and small powers alike, although
the latter – e.g., Sweden, Switzerland – are usually saved from the hubris
of the former by virtue of their relative impotence.[3] Nations and nation-
states do not make plausible Christ-figures, even in metaphorical terms,
because nations are not persons but impersonal aggregates of power, and
power is never innocent and never can be innocent, even when rulers
are relatively good and motivations are relatively pure. In every conceivable respect, the concept of the Christ-nation is both a falsehood and a
folly.

In every conceivable respect, including that of Christianity itself, this
judgment stands. Adam Mickiewicz, it is worth recalling (Chapter I), was
castigated by other nineteenth-century Polish Catholics for abusing
Christian symbols in his romantic glorification of Poland as a crucified
nation. Most probably his critics were as patriotic as the national bard
himself, but they knew that to transform the tragic fate of the Polish
commonwealth into a reprise of the passion of Christ was both idolatrous
and blasphemous. Their indictment was valid in spite of the role that the
romantic vision of the Christ-nation played in keeping alive the dream
of Polish freedom throughout the black periods of political subjugation,
including the terrible Nazi era. In a similar vein, the poetic identification
of contemporary Palestine with Christ (Chapter V), however efficacious
as a means of Palestinian survival, falsifies both historical reality and the
nature of the religion from which the image of crucifixion is drawn. The
crucified nation motif is more than a fool's phantasmagoria, but it is still
a fool's phantasmagoria. Idolatry and blasphemy arise when the glory of
the true Christ is confused with the glory of earthly institutions that bear
his name. churches, states, societies and cultures. The anti-Mickiewicz,
anti-romantic Polish Catholics were not the first Christians to understand
this fact; it was a cardinal insight of the Protestant Reformation. Martin
Luther, a man of many failings, nevertheless saw human nature clearly
when he contrasted the theology of the cross (*theologia crucis*) with the
theology of glory (*theologia gloriae*). In Christian terms, the theology of
the cross totally negates any attempt to glorify the crucified nation, any
crucified nation, Catholic or Protestant, Christian or non-Christian. It is
one of the ironies of Protestant history that the German Lutherans
entirely forgot their mentor's warning when they compared their
national situation during the Great War to that of Jesus at Gethsemane.

---

* The same, of course, is true of other belief-systems, including the secular and atheistic
'heavens' of the fallen National Socialist and Marxist worldviews of recent memory.

Some nations, of course, have really been 'crucified,' as it were, in the bloodbaths of history, and their national immolations invariably tempt their partisans to elevate them above and beyond all other wronged and tortured nations. No other human entity, some Irish nationalists liked to claim (Chapter IV), has ever endured the pain and oppression inflicted on the Irish people, with the possible exception of the Jews. The caveat, however, was reluctant; why except the Jews. Self-pity feeds self-exaltation, the narcissistic belief that one's own national community alone deserves special moral status, a notion that has far more in common with the theology of glory than the theology of the cross, although the theme of crucifixion is its matrix. In the Christian faith, the cross of Christ is most profoundly understood when it is seen as a warning against all forms of idolatry, including Christian idolatry, in fact especially Christian idolatry. "The cross," the twentieth-century Protestant theologian Paul Tillich once declared, "symbolizes the conquest of the demonic temptation to power that we meet in every religion, in every religious leader, and in every priest."[4] Seen in this light, the central symbol of Christianity stands radically and paradoxically opposed to Christianity, or more precisely to Christendom, meaning the temporal embodiment of the Christian religion in the social, political and cultural institutions of the world. As a son of Germany and an academic refugee from Hitler's Third Reich, Tillich learned this lesson at first hand. Not only priests and religious leaders but also leaders of every type and hue, Christian and non-Christian, who turn their conflicts into holy wars always stand on unholy ground themselves. Narcissism, from the Greek myth of Narcissus, the erotic self-love of the flesh, was redefined as *superbia* by St. Augustine, the most subtle and insidious of the sins of the spirit. Its presence in the annals of nationalism is legion.

This does not mean, however, that every instance of nationalist feeling in the modern age is ridden with the same moral hazards as the worst examples, although it does mean that no nationalism is ever safe from corruption. Nationalism has its defenders, even among Christian theologians, who see at least as much good as evil in its manifestations. To the Canadian Catholic theologian Gregory Baum, for example, nationalism is a "polymorphous phenomenon," that is to say a force with more than a single configuration, so that it can serve as a healing balm for broken and oppressed peoples, binding up their psychic and social wounds.[5] Accordingly, one can speak in positive terms of "ethical nationalism" or moral nationalism, an elixir able to change the dross of history into molten gold if the time is auspicious in the evolution of a particular nation and if its alchemists guard against the misuse and abuse of their polymorphous remedy.[6] To be sure, as already acknowledged, the romantic Polish poets (Chapter I), however pretentious their conceits, helped to saved the Poles from joining the lost nationalities of the world, although simple patriotic verse alone might have served this end equally well. To be sure also, the nationalist poets of contemporary Palestine (Chapter V) have helped to foster the Palestinian sense of collective identity during the long siege that endless war has imposed on a still subjugated and dispossessed people: the dialectic of suffering and resistance immortalized by the now celebrated *Intifada*. However, even ethical nationalism cannot be regarded as purely ethical, despite its healing powers; the dark and dangerous side is always its *volte-face*. Only a hair's breadth separates Herder's cosmopolitanism from Fichte's chauvinism, and not much more than a hair's breadth separates the national idealism of Charles Péguy from the national egotism of Jules Michelet (Chapter II) or, for that matter, Charles Maurras and Jean-Marie Le Pen, the mutual devotees of Jeanne d'Arc. There is also the sorry fact that suicide bombers are born and bred in the same ethos as the children of the stone.

Even when it is a force for the good, therefore, the nationalist cure for the ills of the world threatens to become a force for ill. When the cure takes the form of the Christ-nation in Christian or quasi-Christian societies, or in societies such as Palestine that contain a Christian minority, this threat is multiplied. As biblical scholars know, the New Testament narrative of the passion, when presented uncritically, is full of moral pitfalls since blame for the crucifixion is assigned to certain actors in the drama who play certain parts that have become reified not only in scripture itself but also in the long popular memory of historic Christendom: Judas, Caiaphas, Pilate, the Jewish mob, the Roman soldiers. Again, as biblical (and literary) scholars know, these figures are easily demonized, except, of course, the Pilate of the Fourth Gospel who drapes himself in the robes of a philosopher and inquires into the nature of truth.★ This type of characterization is always fraught with peril, especially when the villains of the passion play, like villains in every drama, turn into archetypal figures. Has not Judas, the essential Jew in the antisemitic mind, played a fateful role in the tortured chronicles of the Jewish people, culminating in the holocaust of the twentieth century? When a nation becomes a Christ-nation, when the passion drama is lifted from the pages of the New Testament and transposed onto the canvass of modern history, the moral dangers embedded in the text are brought into sharp and towering relief. A crucified nation requires crucifiers, and

★ John 18:38.

the crucifying powers, like Judas, Caiaphas and Pilate in the New Testament, are assigned nefarious roles as the agents of evil, resulting in their stigmatization and condemnation.

Who crucified Poland, who crucified France, who crucified Germany, who crucified Ireland, who crucified Palestine? The answers are well known and the guilty parties and guilty nations are portrayed as diabolical in the eyes of the victim nation and its propagandists. Poland was crucified by Austria, Prussia and Russia with France ("Gaul") cast as Pontius Pilate. France was crucified by its own traitors, especially the upstart Napoleon III and his minions (cast as Roman soldiers), and by England and Germany. Germany was crucified by France, England (Sadducees and Pharisees) and Russia. Ireland was crucified by England and decadent Irishmen in collusion with England, or conversely by the Catholic pharoah (the pope) and his local agents. Palestine was crucified by Britain and the Zionists, and is still being tortured and crucified by Israel, the Zionist state.

Inherent in this schema is an overwhelming sense of innocence: Christ was innocent – and righteousness; Christ was righteous – with all of the certitudes that innocence entails. The crucified are thus separated in kind as well as in degree from the crucifiers. To innocence and righteousness one can add beauty, another signal attribute of the virtuous soul. Virtue wearing a crown of thorns, guiltlessness pierced in the side and gushing blood, freedom on the rack, marked the extraordinary and tragic fate of the Polish Christ-nation. Nobility of spirit and glorious freedom with gall and vinegar pressed to her lips, the principle of universal life crushed by the power of tyranny, the light of the world extinguished by the cruel alien enemies of light and love, marked the torments of the French Christ-nation. Piety encircled by impious forces suffused with jealousy and hatred of God's *Favoritvolk* marked the Gethsemane of the German Christ-nation, the realm of devout kings and emperors. Suffering unlike the suffering of any other people on earth except the Jews, sacrifice after sacrifice after sacrifice until the whole of its history became a passion play, marked the Irish Christ-nation, at least in one of its incarnations. In the other, political and religious freedom besieged by political and religious obscurantism and tyranny provided the christological frame. Paradisal beauty and harmony violated and ravaged by harsh, soulless and murderous intruders marked the tribulations of the Palestinian Christ-nation. Innocence, virtue and beauty (France, Ireland and Palestine conceived as beautiful women by the romantic imagination) thus define the victim peoples that history has cruelly placed on the cross: the great martyr-nations of the modern age.

Martyrdom, however, is partly a matter of perception, and perception, as our case studies demonstrate, is notoriously one-sided. To describe the First World War as a German "Gethsemane" in disregard of the vast state-of-the-art military might possessed by imperial Germany, the creation in large measure of the military genius Helmuth von Moltke, offends the modern ear, German and non-German alike. Such designations never fail to distort and falsify even when they possess a faint modicum of truth. They also generate an inordinate collective blindness that can and often does lead to terrible deeds. Piosity, on the one hand and blood-thirstiness on the other are the twin characteristics of some of the most potent nationalist movements of our day. The sentimental and sanctimonious Patrick Pearse is by no means the only or even the worst example.

In the final analysis, this collective blindness is the most serious effect of every form of moral dualism. It is the poisoned fruit of every uncritical poetic and sermonic exemption of one's own nation from the sins and vices of other nations, claiming illusory special properties that serve to mute the voice of conscience when crimes are committed in the name of the national cause. A crucified nation rarely if ever dwells on its own failings; it tends instead to dwell on its own victimization and pain, creating a moral hiatus between itself and its crucifiers. This is especially the case when the language of myth is employed, perpetuating the negative images foisted on national foes from time immemorial, as the notorious fratricidal wars of the Balkans pitting Christian against Muslim, Serb against Albanian, etc., are ample proof. While the passage of time and the healing arts can cure even the most deep seated enmities – between France and Germany, between republican Ireland and England, between the two Irelands, perhaps between Israel and Palestine – for example – reconciliation between national communities is a slow and arduous process subject to many disruptions, especially when old obsessions come into play.

There is, moreover, a major complication. Crucified nations are born of humiliation, as Poland was humiliated by Austria, Prussia and Russia, France was humiliated by mediaeval England and modern Germany, Germany was humiliated by Napoleon and the Western Allies, Ireland was humiliated by England, Palestine was humiliated by Israel. As a result, they are either weak or conceive of themselves as weak even if and when they acquire strength at a later period. When biblical and quasi-biblical attributes such as election, messianic identity, providential favour, are attached to the huge powers of a modern nation-state, national self-righteousness and all of its moral pitfalls become rampant; when in addition the nation-state regards itself or is regarded by its children as a crucified nation, an arch-victim of history heinously wronged by other nations, these pitfalls are greatly magnified. Hence the Christ-nation, despite its facile religious allure, is an invidious concept. Whereas Christ himself forgave his crucifiers,* nation-states, which are not persons (in spite of the romantic imagination) in any case, are far less inclined and less able to forgive. They almost always seek vengeance.

Vengeance, however, is a less than noble ideal, and the poets and preachers who wrote and spoke in dark times thought of their nations in noble terms. If they endowed their partisan loyalties with a holy aura, it was because they themselves were deeply embittered by the sad plight of their national communities. Therefore they probably should not be judged too severely. Adam Mickiewicz should not be judged too severely for exalting the Polish nation as a Christ-nation after its literal dissolution toward the close of the eighteenth century; Poland in fact really was crucified. Friedrich Schleiermacher should not be judged too severely for depicting the German struggle against Napoleon as a holy war; the German territories in fact had been overrun and occupied by French armies. Victor Hugo should be judged too severely for depicting France as the Christ of the peoples; Paris, the city of light, was bombarded by the invading Prussians and its streets actually ran with streams of blood during the slaughter of the communards. William Butler Yeats should not be judged too severely for virtually deifying the Irish nation in his nationalistic play *Cathleen ni Houlihan*; the Irish masses in fact were denigrated and effectively allowed to starve during the great potato famine. Ian Paisley should not be judged too severely for portraying Protestant Ulster as the besieged true people of God; the bombs of the Irish Republican Army did much to fortify this ascription. The Palestinian bards should not be judged too severely for portraying Palestine as a nation on the cross; the catastrophe of *al-Nakba* and the sorrows of the refugee camps lend credence to this representation, as does the Israeli occupation and the techniques of control employed by the occupying forces.[7] Hence the crucifixion motif cannot be nullified entirely, despite its distorting and falsifying propensities. It is a powerful but misleading metaphor invariably carried too far by those who employ it, resulting in the illusions already noted. Moreover, it invests nationalism with a religious essence, draping the mantle of the sacred over both the nation and its history. Since nothing is as bad as bad religion, this is always a serious concern.

---

* Luke 23:34.

Sacral nations do not require state churches or official religious designations; they can be secular and anti-clerical and even atheistic as in the case of communist Russia during the Soviet era. Republican France is a secular state, yet the French cult of the nation, according to David A. Bell, remains strangely Catholic in its substance despite the abolition of the old first estate (the Catholic hierarchy) with the French monarchy by the rationalist ideologues of the 1789 revolution.[8] Jeanne d'Arc is a Catholic saint, but she is also the mystical personification of France, a female Christ-figure even to secular republicans such as Jules Michelet. Not only the French right with its Marian pietism but also the French left with its anti-clerical animus is still in some strange way 'Catholic' below the surface of the national culture because Catholicism is closely interwoven with the French national identity, especially in the aesthetic sense.[9] It was the Catholic Church that once mediated the fusion between Roman civilization and the Germanic traditions of ancient Gaul: the treasured French Latin heritage. Hence Jews and Protestants were regarded as aliens during much of the Third Republic despite the egalitarian doctrines promulgated by the Enlightenment and adopted by the revolution. The secular mind only had to substitute racial terms for religious terms in order to practice discrimination. Today, the designated aliens are mostly north African Muslim immigrants. This does not mean, of course, that Catholic Christianity *per se* is racist; the exact opposite is the case. It only means that Catholic themes and symbols have insinuated themselves into the very texture of French nationalism, with not altogether salutary results. Churches are not nations and nations are not churches, but nation-states that become sacral communities function as surrogate churches for those who confuse the glory of God with the glory of the nations.

Christian themes and symbols were also incorporated into the texture of German nationalism, only in a Protestant rather than a Catholic mode. Ever since Luther defied Charles V by refusing to recant in early sixteenth-century Saxony, a visible Protestant thread has run through German history, culminating in the Christian empire established by Bismarck in 1871 with its close alliance between the altar and the throne. The sacral significance of this alliance was greatly magnified by Bismarck's cultural war (*Kulturkampf*) against the independent powers of the churches (especially the Roman Catholic Church) and against the relics of political liberalism in the German state. Holy Germany thus became holier still, the Christ-nation of the romantic nationalists with its God-filled sacred history that not even the demise of the Second Reich in 1918 and the rise of pronounced secular and socialist ideas in militant opposition to Christianity could eradicate. It was in this post-war context that Luther, who lived long before the advent of modern nationalism, was elevated to the status of a Germanic national hero, a nationalist icon, indeed, nothing less than a type of German 'saviour.'[10] This was the work of nationalistic scholars involved in a renaissance of Luther studies, but it acquired a public resonance as a result of the crisis into which national humiliation and paranoiac stab-in-the-back theories had plunged the insecure new Weimar Republic. As the courageous warrior-maid had defied the enemies of France, so the courageous Saxon monk had defied the enemies of Germany, the pope and the Hapsburg emperor, although, unlike his French counterpart, Luther did not perish at the stake. Yet his life could well have ended in martyrdom had the reformer not been protected by Frederick the Wise, the Elector of Saxony. If he had died a martyr, the saviour-redeemer of Germany who knew no more of modern nationalism than Jeanne d'Arc, almost certainly would have found a similar apotheosis in the nationalist pantheons of the twentieth century.

Apotheosis is not too strong a word. The element of the sacred cannot be banished from the social order, no matter how secular the mood of the modern (and post-modern) age. In some manner the religious dimension of human existence will disclose its presence; something, whether the mystique of nationhood, the institutions of statehood, or the glorious moments and glorious men and women in the saga of the nation, will be consecrated and worshipped. Every national community has its larger-than-life heroic figures and every national myth inflates their heroism, aggrandizing them at times almost beyond human recognition. There are, of course, other iconic heroes no less revered in other countries than Jeanne d'Arc in France and Martin Luther in Germany. An obvious example is Abraham Lincoln in the United States. Another famous example is the nineteenth-century poet Taras Shevchenko in the Ukraine, the man who is credited with resurrecting the Ukrainian language and the Ukrainian national consciousness when both were being ground under the heel of imperial Russia: a moving tale of another crucified nation. To insult the much adored and much eulogized Shevchenko, as one iconoclastic Kiev journalist discovered in 2003, is to desecrate the body politic itself, never a safe thing to do in any society.[11] Even more than Mickiewicz in Poland, Shevchenko is regarded as the spiritual liberator of his country, a writer whose verse moulded the national soul. He is therefore a holy figure as al-Qassam in Palestine and many others are holy figures, once again demonstrating the numinous power of the sacred and its tremendous potency for good or ill. Were this not the case, the theme of the crucified nation would be innocent and harmless instead of idolatrous and fraught with moral peril. There is never a large space between the holy and the demonic.

Today, in our warring age, crucified nations abound, and no doubt more will make their entrance onto the historical stage. We began by speaking of the 'Passion of America' (Introduction). Some now speak of the passion of Iraq, another crucified nation with its own sad litany of victimization and symbols of martyrdom which the ongoing bloodletting can only serve to amplify.[12] Other instances are legion: Armenians, Jews,★ Romany (who are often compared to the Jews), Kurds, Kampucheans, Chechnyans, Rwandans, Bosnians, with their variant accounts of discrimination, persecution and mass murder. In Canada the Francophone province of Quebec is seen by one school of indigenous nationalism as a victim nation crucified by the British Empire following the Battle of the Plains of Abraham (1759) and re-crucified by its Anglo-Canadian heirs to the present day. This is subsumed in the popular myth of the conquest which, like all such political myths, is both true and false at the same time. Also in Canada or what later became Canada the French-speaking Acadians (*les Acadiéns*) constitute another crucified nation, having been driven from the maritime regions following their transfer to British hands during the colonial wars of the eighteenth century. Some of their descendants later returned, nursing searing memories that still cast a shadow on local Anglo-French relations. The commonly designated First Nations in Canada, or the aboriginal peoples, also can be deemed a crucified nation – some of their spokesmen certainly believe so – although they do not comprise a single geopolitical entity but rather an amalgam of communities and cultures. These festering wounds are internal exceptions to that otherwise rather mild state of mind usually identified with popular Canadian nationalism, that is to say a romantic and sometimes almost mystical love of all things northern: the proverbial and faintly racial "true north strong and free." Only a northern country would choose a maple leaf as its national emblem.

While the many crucifixion stories of the world are by no means equivalent on the scales of iniquity – there is a huge disparity between the fate of Rwanda and the fate of Quebec, for example – they fall into a common pattern: the crucified and the crucifiers. Not only does this neat and simple distinction between the good and the bad reveal the tyranny of fixed ideas, whether nationalist, racial, tribal, religious or

---

★ Significantly, a Christian historian entitled his 1975 book on the holocaust *The Crucifixion of the Jews*.

utopian, but it also stifles thought and hinders effective action. Nonetheless the motif of the crucified nation has a perennial and toxic appeal.

Notes

1 David A. Bell, *The Cult of the Nation in France: Inventing Nationalism 1680–1800*, Cambridge, Mass.: Harvard University Press, 2001, p. 22.

2 It has been argued that seventeenth-century German pietism was historically related to later German nationalism. (See Koppel S. Pinson, *Pietism as a Factor in the Rise of German Nationalism*, New York: Columbia University Press, 1934.) Paul Tillich often spoke of nationalism as a secular religion or "quasi-religion." (See his study *Christianity and the Encounter of World Religions*, New York: Columbia University Press, 1963.)

3 See *Many are Chosen: Divine Election and Western Nationalism,* William R. Hutchison & Hartmut Lehmann (eds), Minneapolis: Fortress Press, 1994.

4 *Ultimate Concern: Tillich in Dialogue*, D. Mackenzie Brown (ed.), New York: Harper & Row, 1965, p. 136. See also Tillich's analysis of the element of self-negation in the Christian understanding of divine revelation (*Systematic Theology*, Chicago: University of Chicago Press, 1951, Vol. I, pp. 133–134).

5 Gregory Baum, *Nationalism, Religion and Ethics*, Montreal & Kingston: McGill–Queen's University Press, 2001, p. 3.

6 Ibid., p. 31. Baum cites Martin Buber and Mahatma Gandhi as preeminent examples of ethical nationalism.

7 As described by Sari Nusseibeh, *Once Upon a Country: A Palestinian Life*, New York: Farrar, Straus & Giroux, 2007.

8 Bell, op. cit., p. 24. This historical verdict was never reversed, even by Napoleon's concordat with the pope.

9 Charles Maurras, for example, an agnostic, attached great importance to the *Roman* character of Roman Catholicism which he regarded as intrinsic to the French racial genius.

10 See James M. Stayer, *Martin Luther, German Saviour: German Evangelical Theological Factions and the Interpretation of Luther, 1917–1933*, Montreal & Kingston: McGill–Queen's University Press, 2000, p. 17.

11 *Globe and Mail* (Toronto), June 10, 2003. For an interesting analysis of Shevchenko as a national icon, see Anna Makolkin, *Name, Hero, Icon: Semiotics of Nationalism through Heroic Biography*, Berlin: Mouton de Gruyter, 1992.

12 See David Baran, "Falluja: Iraq's place of sacrifice," *Le Monde diplomatique* (December 2004), p. 16.

Index